THE COTSWOLD WAY

About the Author

Kev Reynolds, author of this guide, is a freelance writer, photojournalist and lecturer who lives in the Kent countryside when not trekking or climbing in distant mountain regions. A prolific compiler of guidebooks, his first title for Cicerone Press appeared in 1978 (*Walks & Climbs in the Pyrenees* – now in its fourth edition); this is his 25th book for the same publisher, with others being researched at present. A member of the Alpine Club, Austrian Alpine Club and Outdoor Writers' Guild, his passion for mountains in particular and the countryside in general remains undiminished after 40 years of activity, and he regularly travels throughout Britain to share that enthusiasm through his lectures. Check him out at **www.kevreynolds.co.uk**.

Other UK Cicerone Guides by Kev Reynolds
The Wealdway & The Vanguard Way
Walking in Kent Vols I & II
The South Downs Way
The North Downs Way
Walking in Sussex

THE COTSWOLD WAY

by
Kev Reynolds

2 POLICE SQUARE, MILNTHORPE, CUMBRIA LA7 7PY
www.cicerone.co.uk

Third edition 2007
ISBN-13: 978-1-85284-552-0
© Kev Reynolds 1990, 1994, 2005, 2007
First published 1990
Revised edition 1994
Second edition 2005
ISBN-10: 1-85284-449-3
A catalogue record for this book is available from the British Library
Photos by the author

This book is for my wife, with thanks for her constant loving support, without which I'd still be working from Monday to Friday, looking forward to Saturday.

Acknowledgements

To Jo Ronald, Cotswold Way national trail officer, for information, advice and encouragement and, not least, for her efforts (and those of Don Field, alignment officer) in upgrading the route to national trail standards; to the numerous unnamed volunteers who have worked tirelessly over the years to keep the paths open and make the route such a joy to walk; to those who made my overnights at various b&b establishments both welcoming and comfortable; to Derek Roberts, who firs̶t walked the route with me, and especially to my companion for the memorable Cots̶wold days, and many footpath miles, who have walked together; and lastly, to the team at Cicerone who have managed the mapping, and for putting their talents and skills to my advantage. I am grateful to you all.

Kev Reynolds

Front cover: The Devil's Chimney on Leckhampton Hill's steep face has become a symbol of the C

CONTENTS

THE COTSWOLD WAY – BRITAIN'S NEWEST NATIONAL TRAIL

This new edition of *The Cotswold Way* guide has been produced to coincide with the elevation of the route to national trail status in May 2007. Despite the fact that this much-loved long distance trail has been in existence for more than 35 years, as a newly designated national trail it benefits from fresh waymarking and signing, realigned or improved footpaths, and the provision of numerous kissing gates in place of stiles. What remains unchanged is the matchless series of landscapes and idyllic villages that help make the Cotswolds one of Britain's finest regions, and ensure that the 102 mile (164km) journey between Chipping Campden and Bath is a joy from start to finish.

Advice to Readers

Readers are advised that while every effort is taken by the author to ensure the accuracy of this guidebook, changes can occur which may affect the contents. It is advisable to check locally on transport, accommodation, shops, and so on, but even rights of way can be altered. Paths can be affected by forestry work, landslip or changes of ownership.

The author would welcome information on any updates and changes sent through the publishers.

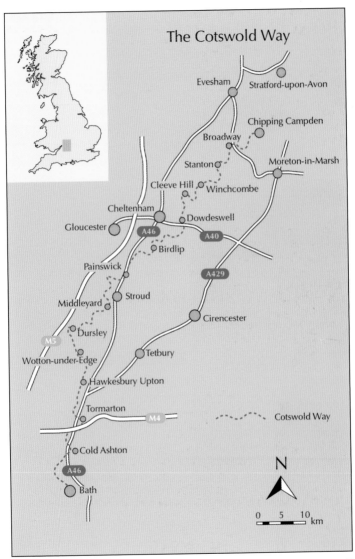

The Cotswold Way

- Stratford-upon-Avon
- Evesham
- Chipping Campden
- Broadway
- Stanton
- Moreton-in-Marsh
- Cleeve Hill
- Winchcombe
- Cheltenham
- Dowdeswell
- Gloucester
- A46
- A40
- Birdlip
- Painswick
- A429
- Middleyard
- Stroud
- Cirencester
- Dursley
- M5
- Tetbury
- Wotton-under-Edge
- Hawkesbury Upton
- Tormarton
- M4
- Cold Ashton
- A46
- Bath

····· Cotswold Way

N

0   5   10 km

Hardwood marker posts guide the route throughout

INTRODUCTION

Views were lost in a grey mist of rain that had not let up since breakfast, but needing a hot drink I sank onto a cushion of heather, settled back against a silver birch and dug my flask out of the rucksack. The tea was welcome; the rain and lack of views had not affected my spirits and I was aware of being immensely happy. It was a privilege to be there, to be walking this land of timeless beauty, absorbing its past and present, gleaning experience for tomorrow's patchwork of memory. And as I wiped the steam from my glasses I noticed, among the swamps of nodding cowslips

that crowded the hillside, early purple orchids standing sentry-like here and there, their helmets tossing minute cascades of spray as raindrops fell upon them ...

The soft light of a June evening pushed shadows out of a stand of beech trees. From a pathside bank I watched the patch of darkness spread down the knoll as silvered galleon clouds drifted overhead and a blackbird piped his own last post from a hawthorn bush nearby. At the foot of the slope a roe deer slipped out of the woodland shaw and sprang across the long grass, as

Ramsons, or wild garlic (Allium ursinum), spreads through the woodlands in great carpets, its beautiful white stars giving contrast to its pungent smell

though leaping waves. Reluctant to break the spell I delayed my onward walk and sat, content to absorb the moment ...

These are just two random vignettes that spill unbidden from a host of memories gathered along the Cotswold Way, but each time I've walked the route end to end – and others when I've snatched isolated sections for the sheer pleasure of being there – I've been seduced by the region's special attractions. There are the curving bays and spurs of the escarpment, the beech-crowned heights, open breezy commons, deeply cut dry valleys, mile upon mile of drystone walling from which anxious wrens dart and where snails cling limpet-like to the verticals. I think of honey-coloured cottages, roses wild and nurtured, carpets of bluebells, ramsons and wood anemones, kestrels hovering head-

down above the cropped turf, larks warbling from dawn to dusk, a cumulus of sheep on the brow of a distant hill. I remember old churches, Civil War battlefields, and the even older burial mounds and hill forts that pepper the route. I recall beams of sunlight shafting onto the River Severn, clouds rolling over the Black Mountains far away. And the peace. Not silence, but peace. The peace of a countryside comfortable with itself.

A walker's landscape is both a powerful stimulant and an inspiration. Certainly that is true where memories and dreams intertwine in a complex of pleasures on completion of the Cotswold Way.

THE COTSWOLD WAY

The Cotswold Way measures 102 miles (164km) on its journey from Chipping Campden to Bath, and it's a devious

The national trail acorn symbol adorns Cotswold Way waymarks and signposts

route – a switchback, stuttering, to-ing and fro-ing, climbing and falling walk. One moment you're wandering along the scarp edge, with toy-sized farms and villages scattered across the plains far below, the next you're heading down to them – to explore a magical village, or a small market town with age in its streets, whose cottages are 'faintly warm and luminous, as if they knew the trick of keeping the lost sunlight of centuries glimmering about them'. Then you head up again, zigzagging back and forth in order to capture the best the wolds can offer.

The wolds form part of an extensive belt of oolitic limestone that runs from Dorset in the south to Yorkshire in the north. The highest and broadest part of this belt is an undulating tableland, raised on its western side and draining gently towards the east, down to the Thames Valley and the Oxfordshire Plain. On its western side, where the Cotswold Way goes, the scarp slope falls abruptly to the Severn Plain, revealing its most dramatic features. This sharp-edged tableland has long jutting prows and spurs, time-moulded coombes and island-like outliers, plateaux fuzzed with woodlands and a grid of drystone walls. Numerous mounds provide evidence of a long history of occupation along the very rim of the escarpment, from which early man scanned the broad views, alert to approaching danger. Today the Cotswold wayfarer seeks those same vantage points as highlights of the

walk, places on which to sprawl in the grass and dream among the flowers.

The Cotswold Way was developed by Gloucestershire County Council as a recreational route following a suggestion made by the district committee of the Ramblers' Association as long ago as the early 1950s. As one of the county council's major initiatives to mark European Conservation Year, the route was eventually launched in May 1970 during National Footpath Week. Five years later its full length was treated to a concentrated effort of waymarking, mainly by volunteers from the RA and the Cotswold Voluntary Warden Service, and it subsequently became one of the most effectively waymarked long-distance walks in Britain.

Now at last it has been recognised as a national trail, and with that recognition comes financial backing – the whole route has been surveyed, evaluated, and in some places realigned. It has been re-signed and waymarked with the acorn symbol, countless stiles have been replaced by kissing gates, and a few sections of footpath have been surfaced where before they were either eroded or boggy.

For this edition of the guide, the Cotswold Way was rechecked in the spring of 2007, just two months before its official launch as a national trail in May. Following information kindly supplied by Jo Ronald, the National Trail Officer responsible for the route, all realignments were walked and assessed, even where improvements and waymarking had yet to be completed. Route descriptions in this guide reflect those changes and, as far as can be ascertained, represent the official course of the Cotswold Way at its national trail launch. Any further necessary improvements will no doubt be posted on the national trail website **www.nationaltrail.co.uk/cotswold** and described in subsequent editions of this guidebook.

Waymarks follow the nationally approved method of using different coloured arrows: yellow for footpaths, blue for bridleways, white for public roads. What differentiates Cotswold Way arrows from other route directions is the black acorn symbol of a national trail (the original CW symbol was a white spot painted on or by the arrowhead, and some of these still exist). Where the route goes through a town, waymarks may be seen on kerbstones, on the posts of traffic direction signs, or on walls. Where it crosses a golf course (on Cleeve Common, Stinchcombe Hill, and Painswick Hill, for example), low wooden waymark posts will be seen. (Note that the original metal signposts along the Cotswold Way give distances in kilometres, while the new national trail posts are measured in miles.)

This is a route, like a number of others, that best repays an unhurried approach. There are so many places of interest nearby that no walker ought to resist the temptation to stray here and there in order to broaden his or her overall view of the region. 'Intently haphazard' is a term which admirably suits this attitude to walking the Cotswold Way.

Chipping Campden makes a worthy beginning, Bath a worthy end. Between the two the way follows a meandering course through woodlands, along the western rim of the escarpment for mile after mile, down into secretive coombes, along the banks of millstreams, over sunny belvederes, exploring one glorious village after another, and always seeking to reveal the very essence of the Cotswolds, the spirit of the region. And it works. It works supremely well.

Which way to walk – north to south, or vice versa? Should you begin in Chipping Campden or Bath?

Well, the route has been signed in such a way as to make it easy to follow in either direction, and there's a similar amount of uphill as there is downhill effort involved, whichever way you tackle it – though if anything it's slightly more strenuous for the northbound walker. By walking northward (starting in Bath) you'll probably have the prevailing wind at your back, some of the finest scenery teasing ahead of you, and one of the finest of all Cotswold towns as the climax.

On the other hand, heading south from Chipping Campden means that from the very start you are launched into full Cotswold grandeur, while the pilgrimage nature of the long- distance walk (and it seems to me that all long walks take the form of a pilgrimage) culminates with the heart-stopping sight of Bath Abbey, arguably one of

Britain's finest buildings, marking journey's end. It is also physically easier to leave Bath by public transport at the end of the walk than it is Chipping Campden. This may be a deciding factor.

Whichever way you choose, both directions are described in this guide.

HOW TO GET THERE

Getting to and from the Cotswold Way by public transport is perfectly straightforward, although some homework may be needed concerning timing. Appendix B gives telephone numbers for train and bus timetable information.

Rail

Train services connect London with Bath (in 90 minutes), as well as Stroud, Cheltenham, Moreton-in-Marsh and Evesham. Stratford-upon-Avon is served by rail from Birmingham. The Birmingham to Bristol line gives an opportunity to reach the Cotswold Way from stations at Ashchurch, Cheltenham, Gloucester, and Cam and Dursley. At the time of writing bus services connect Chipping Campden with the rail network at Evesham, Stratford-upon-Avon and Moreton-in-Marsh.

National Express

National Express coaches serve Bath, Cheltenham and Broadway.

Bus

Bus routes into and along the Cotswolds are operated by several companies, but

since operators are free to change or cancel services provided they give six weeks' notice to the county councils, it is not possible to give any real indication of service provision here. For national bus timetable information ☎0870 608 2608.

ACCOMMODATION

Although the Cotswold Way can be walked in dislocated day sections with the aid of private (and, in some cases, public) transport, this guide has been written with the long-distance walker in mind. Overnight accommodation along the way is therefore a prime concern, and I have indicated where such accommodation was available during research, but for current details you are advised to obtain a copy of a first-rate publication compiled by the Gloucestershire Area Ramblers' Association. *The Cotswold Way Handbook & Accommodation List* details existing accommodation on or near the route, giving addresses, telephone numbers, grid references, and so on, of a range of private b&bs, hotels and pubs. This highly recommended publication, which is updated and published annually, may be purchased from the Ramblers' Association whose London address is found in Appendix A.

The Ramblers' Association also publishes details of bed-and-breakfast accommodation throughout the country, as recommended by its members, and listed under county sections. *The Ramblers' Yearbook and*

13

South of the Battlefields, on Lansdown Hill, green hills fold into a tight valley (Section 13 southbound, section 1 northbound)

Accommodation Guide is published annually, comes free with membership, and includes facilities along the Cotswold Way.

Walkers are advised to book their accommodation in advance, and note that beds are at a premium during the race week of the Cheltenham Festival (in March), and when the Badminton Horse Trials take place (late April/May).

It should also be noted that there are very few facilities for campers along the Cotswold Way, although a few bed-and-breakfast establishments do allow camping in their grounds (see *The Cotswold Way Handbook* for details). Should you be eager to carry a tent, it is important to seek the landowner's permission before pitching it.

RECOMMENDED MAPS

Map sections illustrated in this guide are taken from the Ordnance Survey's Landranger series at a scale of 1:50,000 (1¼ inches: 1 mile or 2cm = 1km).

Start and finish points for each route section are marked on the maps, together with a symbol at the start point to indicate the direction of the route – southbound or northbound (see key below).

While the maps in this guide show each stage of the route, walkers are recommended to consult the sheets from which they are taken, or other maps as detailed below, in order to gain a wider picture of the landscape, and to locate overnight accommodation which may not appear on the

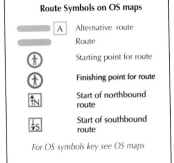

Route Symbols on OS maps

A — Alternative route

— Route

🚶 Starting point for route

🚶 **Finishing point for route**

Start of northbound route

Start of southbound route

For OS symbols key see OS maps

USING THE GUIDE

For the majority of the route, waymarking and signposts should be sufficient to make detailed guidebook descriptions superfluous. But in case of doubt, or if a crucial waymark or sign is missing, the route is described as found on my most recent walking of it in its entirety in 2004, with re-routed sections checked in the spring of 2007. However, upgrading to national trail status has led to a few more sections being highlighted for re-routing and improvement in the future. Should any of these new sections be opened during the lifetime of this guidebook's printing, they will no doubt be given plenty of signing, so if you find that the route described here varies from that on the ground, you are advised to follow the waymarked alternative (if, of course, the waymark bears the CW symbol).

Notification of any major changes along the way will be borne in mind for future editions of this guidebook, and a postcard detailing any variations, errors or anomalies, sent to me via the publisher, will be greatly appreciated.

For the purpose of this guide, the route has been divided into 13 separate sections dictated by the existence of overnight accommodation. The longest of these is 10 miles (16km), the shortest 6 miles (9½km). How many days you take to walk the full 102 miles (164km) is down to personal choice, of course, but by doubling some of these stages, the Cotswold Way could be walked in as little as five days for those prepared to average a little over 20 miles (32km)

limited strip maps published here. Five Landranger sheets cover the length of the Cotswold Way: numbers 150, 151, 162, 163 and 172. But for greater detail you may prefer to use the OS Explorer series at a scale of 1:25,000 (2½ inches = 1 mile or 4cm = 1km). Again, five of these sheets will be needed for the complete Cotswold Way: numbers OL45, 155, 167, 168 and 179.

Perhaps the most convenient mapping of the route, however, is that published by Harvey Maps at a scale of 1:40,000 (a fraction over 1½ inches: 1 mile, or 2½cm = 1km). The single sheet 'Cotswold Way' depicts the route on seven strip maps, each of which is contained within an individual fold. Printed on waterproof paper, the sheet also contains additional information, plus street maps showing the route in detail through Chipping Campden and Bath. The only limitation of Harvey's Cotswold Way map is the restricted amount of country shown beyond the route's corridor.

per day, although this is most definitely a route to be walked at a leisurely pace. As a rough guide, for a route of this length about 2½ miles (4km) an hour will probably be maintained by most regular walkers. When calculating how long any given stage is likely to take, do not forget to include time for rests, photography, consulting the map or guidebook, studying something of particular interest, or admiring a view – all of which add substantially to the day's activity. In hot, wet or windy conditions your pace is likely to be slower than normal, so take the weather into account too.

At the beginning of the description of each section of the route, you will find the distance quoted in miles and kilometres (metric equivalents are rounded to the nearest half). Details are given of specific map sheets, and a note of where accommodation and refreshments may be found. Throughout the route text you will find items or places of interest highlighted in bold type, and nearby, in a box, additional information on the subject.

Occasionally grid references are quoted to allow you to locate a given position on the OS map, which is divided by a series of vertical and horizontal lines to create a grid (the British National Grid). Each of these lines is allocated a number which is quoted at the top, bottom and either side of the map sheet. Numbers increase from left to right for vertical lines (eastings), and from bottom to top for horizontal lines (northings).

To identify an exact position on the map from a grid reference, take the first two digits from the six-figure number quoted – these refer to the 'eastings' line on the OS sheet. The third digit is calculated in tenths of the square moving from left to right. Next, take the fourth and fifth digits, which refer to the 'northings' line, and finally take the sixth and last digit to estimate the number of tenths in the northing square moving up the sheet.

THE COTSWOLDS

The landscape

When walking a long-distance route it is useful to know something of its history, and the landscape's background. About 180 million years ago, the region now known as the Cotswolds was covered by a warm, shallow sea. On its bed settled the shells of tiny creatures along with sediments of sand and clay. Over untold millennia these sediments were compressed into the oolitic limestone that was pushed up to form the very backbone of the land, and which provided the stone that has since been used for the construction of countless lovely cottages, manor houses and churches, not to mention the long miles of drystone walling seen almost everywhere.

The Cotswold mass has an eastward tilt, with the sharp face of the escarpment to west and north, and the limestone resting on several thicknesses of soft Lias clays. Thanks to that tilt,

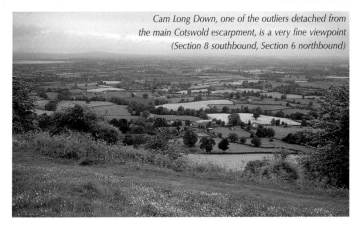

Cam Long Down, one of the outliers detached from the main Cotswold escarpment, is a very fine viewpoint (Section 8 southbound, Section 6 northbound)

natural weathering processes are aided in their slow but steady destruction of the whole area: streams are constantly weakening the scarp slope, the clays slip and overlying rock crumbles without its former support. Thus the scarp has become a corrugation of bays and projecting prows, similar to a coastline, but without the tides of an ocean lapping at its base. Yet even without the wash of tides the scarp is being worn away and pushed further east and south. 'Outliers' such as Cam Long Down near Dursley, Bredon Hill near Evesham, and Dundry Hill to the south of Bristol, provide evidence of the former position of the Cotswold scarp and suggest that the wolds once spread throughout the Severn Vale.

At the end of the last ice age, some 10,000 years ago, the bare bones of the Cotswolds were given a flesh of vegetation. At first, no doubt, the wolds would have been colonised by deciduous woodlands, but in Neolithic times clearings were made and primitive forms of agriculture attempted on the virgin land. With successive generations the open spaces grew until, by the Middle Ages, the Cotswolds were one vast sheepwalk. Then the process of agricultural evolution exchanged pasture for arable land and, following the Enclosures smaller fields were created. Now, it appears, the wheels of evolution are turning once more.

To the flower-loving wayfarer Cotswold limestone brings a rich treasury of orchids (green-winged and early purple in late April and May, common spotted, pyramid, musk, bee and frog in the full flush of summer), harebells and cowslips in the meadows, wild garlic (ramsons) massed with bluebells in damp, shaded woodlands in springtime, following a green carpet of dog's mercury towards the end of winter.

In April Standish Wood is carpeted with bluebells (Section 7 southbound, Section 7 northbound)

Cleeve Common contains the highest land on the Cotswold Way, at over 1000ft (300m), and is one of the last remaining ancient grasslands. As many as 150 species of herbs and grasses may be found there, and it is now a grade 1 site of special scientific interest.

White oxeye daises are abundant among the grasslands. Bird's-foot trefoil, scabious, kidney vetch, thyme, salad burnet and hoary plantain, rock-rose and knapweeds all combine to provide a tapestry of colour, while the hedgerows are often tangled with wild clematis (old man's beard), and clumps of hawthorn shower the slopes with a froth of bloom in springtime.

Bullfinches and yellow hammers flash to and fro among the hawthorn bushes, alternating between thorn bush and gorse. Woodpeckers rattle the deadwoods, buzzards and kestrels hang seemingly motionless high above open hill slopes, alert for any sign of voles or mice far below. Pheasants will almost certainly threaten the unwary with heart failure as they practically explode from under your boots as you wander along the overgrown edge of a field, or through a woodland in autumn. Deer may be sighted in some of the larger woodlands and, with a short detour from the way into Dyrham Park, there's a large herd of fallow deer, reckoned to be one of the oldest in Britain, while foxes and badgers, rabbits, hares and countless grey squirrels may all be seen along the way.

Man in the landscape

Man in the landscape could well be the walk's theme. As we have seen, the Cotswolds have no vast wilderness, no

18

raw mountains or trackless moorland; it is not a countryside that threatens or bullies, but one that welcomes. Man has lived in harmony with nature for a long time here, using as a basic building material the very substance of the land, exhibiting a rare degree of artistry in the moulding of wall, doorway and crooked roof, until even the villages themselves appear to be an extension of that land, an integral part of the landscape.

Instead of shunning habitation, as do many other long-distance paths, the Cotswold Way actively seeks out the timeless villages and towns that are among the loveliest features of the region. But timeless though they may seem, they are only comparatively recent additions to a landscape that has been worked, in some form or another, for 5000 years and more.

The first Cotsallers were nomads, hunter-gatherers who drifted through what was then a heavily wooded region, but made little visual impact upon it. It was Neolithic man, around 3000BC, who first began to clear patches in the woodland cover and to till the soil, and in so doing started a primitive form of landscape management. These groups of New Stone Age agriculturalists left behind some 85 burial tombs scattered throughout the region, among the finest being Hetty Pegler's Tump and Belas Knap, both on

The way into Stanton passes this charming thatched cottage (Section 1 southbound, Section 13 northbound)

or very close to the Cotswold Way. These ancient relics are typical of what has become known as the Severn-Cotswold Group: large cairns of stone with a covering of soil, and internal passageways lined with drystone walling which open into burial chambers. It has been estimated that some of these tombs must have involved about 15,000 man-hours to build, which indicates a surprising level of social involvement and organisation.

As well as Hetty Pegler's Tump and Belas Knap, there is another similar burial mound of the same period on Frocester Hill, while at Crickley Hill near Birdlip recent excavations reveal evidence of a 3 acre (1¼ hectares) Neolithic causewayed camp. This contained a village protected by earthwork defences of a double ditch and dry walling topped by a palisade. The discovery of flint arrowheads and items of charred fencing suggest that life in the New Stone Age was not entirely peaceful.

Neolithic man was replaced by tribes of immigrants from the Low Countries. These so-called 'Beaker People' of the Bronze Age lived a mostly nomadic existence, raising stock and undertaking a primitive form of cultivation before moving on. The most significant evidence of their occupation of the Cotswolds (though these are not always clearly visible) is in the form of round barrows, contrasting with the long barrows in which their predecessors had buried their dead. Although there are more than 350 of these round barrows, none of any importance are actually to be seen along the Cotswold Way.

What is visible, however, is a series of hill and promontory forts dating from the Iron Age, which lasted from about 700BC until the Roman occupation. The work of Belgic immigrants known as Dobunni, it is thought that these defended enclosures served different purposes. Some clearly contained working communities with villages of long houses, some were market centres or animal corrals, and some of the smaller enclosures perhaps were the fortified homes of Dobunni tribal chieftains. Yet whatever their function, they conformed to set patterns, being protected by deep, rock-cut ditches and tall, near-vertical walls. Nowadays they invariably appear as rounded, grass-covered mounds, some saucer-shaped and distinctive, others perhaps with sections of wall having been lost under centuries of ploughing. There are many fine examples of these hill forts along the route, the largest being at Little Sodbury, where Sodbury Hill Fort covers 11 acres (4½ hectares), enclosed by ditches and earth ramparts. Uleybury is even larger, at more than 30 acres (12 hectares), but is just off the route. Set on the escarpment above Dursley it had the additional protection of a 300ft (90m) drop down the scarp face. Other hill forts may be seen along the way on Cleeve Common, Leckhampton Hill, Crickley Hill and Painswick Beacon, among others.

When the Romans came in AD43 they adopted some of these Iron Age

*The Roman baths, near Bath Abbey
(Section 13 southbound, Section 1 northbound)*

camps for their own use. In addition they built a fortress at Cirencester and another near Gloucester, then linked the two with Ermin Street, which is met on the Cotswold Way at Birdlip. Away from the towns – and none is greater in this part of Britain than the world heritage city of Bath – agricultural estates were established and well-to-do citizens built villas for themselves, usually richly decorated with mosaics, on well-chosen sites that caught the sun. The Cotswold Way passes near two of these, one above Wadfield Farm near Winchcombe, the other at Witcombe below Cooper's Hill.

The Roman occupation of the Cotswolds ended in AD410 with the withdrawal of the legions and the advance of the Saxons. The Dark Ages that followed are shrouded in mystery, but it is thought that these latest newcomers brought with them a way of life that was not ordered with the same degree of Roman culture and organisation, and there seem to have been many tribal differences to settle. It was during this period that Arthur rose as defender of Britain. Tales of King Arthur are a muddle of historic evidence and legend, but that these were unsettled times cannot be in doubt. What seems certain is that towards the end of the sixth century a battle took place on Hinton Hill, near Dyrham, between West Saxon warlords Cuthwine and Cealwin, and three kings of the Britons. The kings – Coinmail, Condidan and Farinmail – were slaughtered and the Britons pushed back to Wales and Somerset leaving the towns of Bath, Cirencester and Gloucester in Saxon hands.

The Cotswolds were then ruled by West Saxons in the south, and Mercian Saxons in the north. The Mercian capital was established at Winchcombe where a monastery was founded. At the abbey at Bath, which became an important and substantial Saxon town, King Edgar was crowned the first King of all England in AD973. The Church grew in power, and by the end of the Saxon period actually owned a good proportion of the Cotswolds. It was during this period that whole sheep-skins were being exported to serve English missionaries on the continent, an export that began as early as AD700.

Under Norman rule, following the invasion of 1066, the Cotswolds remained a place of some importance in the country, with England's capital being very briefly centred at Gloucester. A new phase of building began, evidence of which can still be seen today, particularly in the churches. Horton Court, a few yards off the route of the Cotswold Way, also dates from Norman times and is still in use.

The Domesday Survey of 1086 showed that the region was already largely cultivated, but with woodland covering much of the western escarpment. More clearings were made during the following centuries and the open fields then turned to extensive sheep pasture. 'In Europe the best wool is English; in England the best wool is Cotswold.' This saying held true throughout the Norman era, when sheep outnumbered people by four to one and exports of Cotswold wool increased accordingly.

The traditional animal of these vast sheepwalks was known as the Cotswold Lion, a breed of sheep '. . . with the whitest wool, having long necks and square bodies'. These long necks were adorned with a shaggy woollen 'mane', which led to their nickname. By the Middle Ages the wolds were almost entirely given over to grazing these sheep, and the wool masters used their great wealth to build some of the grand houses and elegant churches (complete with lavish stained glass and intricate carvings) that now form such a feature of the Cotswold Way. Chipping Campden owes both its charm and its architectural splendour to the wool masters; its church is a monument built on the proceeds of wool sales, as are those at Wotton-under-Edge and several other places along the route.

The decline in the export of raw wool began in the early 15th century with crippling taxes. (Revenue from wool at one time accounted for more than half of England's fortune.) But this decline was partly addressed by the home manufacture of cloth, when the new masters of the Cotswolds were mill owners and middlemen who built fine houses for themselves in Painswick and the Stroud Valley, taking over from the sheep owners as financiers of a fresh spate of church building, creating a new middle class in the process.

In the 17th century the Civil War was fought here, as elsewhere, forcing a temporary halt in the fortunes that were being made. Along the escarpment several battle sites are passed on the Cotswold Way, among them a hilltop area still known today as the Battlefields, where the Battle of Lansdown was fought on 5 July 1643. At the other end of the walk, Campden House, next to Chipping Campden's parish church, was taken as a garrison for Royalist troops, but when they left in 1645 they destroyed it by fire. Painswick's church still bears signs of a Civil War skirmish, and one of the last of the battles was fought on the slopes of Dover's Hill.

Between 1700 and 1840 large areas of open land were enclosed by Acts of Parliament, which brought about the countryside's greatest change in appearance for hundreds of years. This was when drystone walls and hedges began to divide the wolds into the criss-cross grid patterns we see today. Large estates were planted with shelter belts for the raising of game birds, while the Cotswolds as a whole became much less dependent on sheep and turned instead to a broader agricultural base with arable land replacing the sheepwalks of old.

To all intents and purposes, this is the landscape explored by walkers of the Cotswold Way in the early years of the 21st century.

Music drew me through twilit streets at the end of my first walking of the Cotswold Way. Rounding a corner I saw a busker in an old raincoat leaning against a wall, scraping Mozart from his violin. Directly ahead rose Bath Abbey. Deep in shadow below, bright in floodlight above, it rose out of the darkness into a shaft of white light as a symbol of peace and hope and beauty. Behind me stretched 100 miles and more of wandering through an enchanting, scenic part of Britain, and Bath Abbey represented its completion. The Cotswold Way ended for me as memorably as it had begun. And in between? Well, in between there had been colour, history, romance, peace – an ever-evolving experience through a constantly changing series of landscapes. A walk, it was, of considerable beauty. What more could anyone ask?

May your experience of the Cotswold Way be as rich and memorable as each of mine has been.

And finally, as you set out to walk the Cotswold Way, please remember that the countryside needs your care and respect.

The Country Code

1 Enjoy the countryside and respect its life and work.

2 Guard against all risks of fire.

3 Fasten all gates.

4 Keep dogs under close control.

5 Keep to public paths across farmland.

6 Use gates and stiles to cross fences, hedges and walls.

7 Leave livestock, crops and machinery alone.

8 Take litter home.

9 Help to keep all water clean.

10 Protect wildlife, plants and trees.

11 Take special care on country roads.

12 Make no unnecessary noise.

The Country Code follows in the wake of principles set down by Octavia Hill, a champion of the countryside and one of the founders of the National Trust, who wrote in the early days of the 20th century:

Let the grass growing for hay be respected, let the primrose roots be left in their loveliness in the hedges, the birds unmolested and the gates shut. If those who frequented country places would consider those who live there, they would better deserve and more often retain, the rights and privileges they enjoy.

Trackway through Witcombe Wood
(Section 6 southbound, Section 8 northbound)

INFORMATION AT A GLANCE

Accommodation: See *The Cotswold Way Handbook & Accommodation List* (available from the Ramblers' Association).

Banks: There are banks on the route at Chipping Campden, Broadway, Winchcombe, Dursley, Wotton-under-Edge and Bath.

Clothing & equipment: Take clothing and equipment appropriate for the season. Waterproofs should be carried at all times of the year. Choose comfortable, well-fitting boots. A first-aid kit to deal with minor injuries and blisters is recommended. Carry map, compass and guidebook.

Food: Each of the towns along the way, and most of the villages *en route*, have places where it's possible to buy food or meals.

Maps: OS Landranger maps: 150, 151, 162, 163, 172
OS Explorer 155, 167, 168, 179, OL45
Harvey's Cotswold Way.

Public transport: The nearest rail services for Chipping Campden are at Evesham, Stratford-upon-Avon and Moreton-in-Marsh, each of which is connected to Chipping by bus.
Bath Spa is on the national rail network.
Both Chipping Campden and Bath are served by National Express coaches.

Route information: Check for any route changes on
www.cotswoldway.gov.uk.

Stanton Reservoir (Section 1)

INTRODUCTION

To walk south along the Cotswold Way is to make a pilgrimage with Bath, its Regency splendour and the glory of its abbey, beckoning from afar. Though you may well have the prevailing wind in your face, this should be adequately compensated for by long views and sunshine on your brow. The southbound route is a little less strenuous than walking northward, where there's rather more up than down, and – this is important – when you begin in Chipping Campden the essential harmony of the Cotswolds is with you from the very start.

Before setting out, time should be allowed to explore the town, for there's much to see and admire, to absorb and file away in memory and recall in other towns and villages along the way. Almost as soon as Campden is left behind there are long views to soak in, and the first of many walks along the escarpment, this time to Broadway Tower, then down to Broadway and up again before you reach Stanton and Stanway.

The escarpment is gained and lost countless times on the way to Bath, the first day or two offering a particular abundance of fresh excuses to descend to the plain and then climb up again. There are field paths, woodland trails, old drove-roads and saltways, green lanes and minor roads winding between hedgerows

Leckhampton Hill, a wonderful vantage point above Cheltenham (Section 5)

Drystone walls like this one at the end of the Mile Drive are a feature of the Cotswolds

lively with sparrows and wrens, fragrant with honeysuckle in spring and early summer, and with huge panoramas across the plains.

From Stanway there's an up and down stretch to the ruins of Hailes Abbey and across undulating farmland to Winchcombe, with its pretty cottages, village stocks and gargoyles round the church. After Winchcombe there's Belas Knap (worth half an hour of anyone's time), then on to the highest part of the whole route on Cleeve Common.

Cleeve Common leads to Leckhampton Hill, another lofty belvedere overlooking Cheltenham, with the eye-catching digit of the Devil's Chimney jutting from a lower scarp terrace. South of Leckhampton is Crickley Hill, where history, in the form of a hill fort, lies partly exposed, and an observation platform provides an opportunity to look back 1000 years and more.

Between Crickley Hill and Cooper's Hill the way crosses just below Birdlip, which sits astride the Roman route of the Fosse Way. Woods conceal the broadest views, but the approach to Cooper's Hill still allows plenty to gaze at, with a soft light flooding through the trees. More woods stretch along the escarpment, but the way emerges onto Painswick Beacon, open and green, splashed with silver birch and birdsong. Down then to the whitest of all Cotswold towns. Painswick has a churchyard known far and wide for its table tombs and exquisite yews – but there's much more besides.

From Painswick a climb leads onto Scottsquar Hill and to what many consider the finest vantage point of the whole walk, Haresfield Beacon. This is indeed a

The path below Haresfield Beacon (Section 7)

tremendous knoll from which to gaze out over the Vale of Gloucester, the River Severn and Forest of Dean. After absorbing all you can from here it's back to woodland for a downhill stretch into an industrial valley overlooked by Stroud.

From cloth mills on the River Frome to woodlands hanging from the steep scarp slope takes only an hour or so. Peace and serenity are restored as you regain the escarpment, where huge views look out to a pair of outliers which soon have to be crossed. Near Hetty Pegler's Tump the Cotswold Way plunges down the scarp, then climbs up and over Cam Long Down before swooping down once more – this time into Dursley.

Dursley leads to Stinchcombe Hill, and from there to North Nibley, Nibley Knoll and Wotton-under-Edge. (What names there are to conjure with in the Cotswolds!) Wotton has its millstreams, and the stage beyond Wotton explores a narrow valley lit by a lively little stream that once powered several mills, one of which is passed on the way to Hawkesbury Upton.

Out of Hawkesbury you follow the old trading route of Bath Lane. Tiny Horton is next, closely followed by Little Sodbury and Old Sodbury, through Dodington Park and up to Tormarton sitting pretty on the edge of a motorway hell. Dyrham seems all but forgotten in its leafy dell. Cold Ashton smiles out to the south and, as you leave it along Greenways Lane, so a luxurious bowl of countryside draws you on.

It's not far then to Bath. Over the Battlefields, along the escarpment once more, round a golf course and across an Iron Age hill fort and you come to Prospect Stile, with the first view of Bath lying in its hollow. Best of all is the view onto Kelston Round Hill, one of the finest of all hills seen since leaving Chipping Campden. The onward route leads round its shoulder and down to Regency Bath, along a maze of elegant streets until at last you come face to face with that gem of an abbey. That sight alone is worth walking the Cotswold Way for.

SECTION 1

Chipping Campden to Stanton

Distance	10 miles (16km)
Maps	Harvey's Cotswold Way 1:40,000
	OS Landranger 151 Stratford-upon-Avon & Surrounding Area, and 150 Worcester, the Malverns & Surrounding Area 1:50,000.
	OS Explorer OL45 The Cotswolds 1:25,000
Accommodation	Chipping Campden, Broadway and Stanton
Refreshments	Broadway and Stanton

The walk begins full of promise but with a temptation to delay, for Chipping Campden is surely the loveliest of all Cotswold market towns, packed with architectural gems softened by a golden, honey-coloured stone. This is Cotswold vernacular at its best, but on this first section there will be other places, other villages, similarly destined to slow the pace and tease with delight – Broadway is one, Stanton is another.

As soon as Campden's streets are left behind, the route climbs onto the escarpment where Dover's Hill rewards with a long view across the Vale of Evesham to the distant Malvern Hills. Breaking away from the scarp edge the way continues along what is known as the Mile Drive, over fields and across the A44 on Fish Hill to the base of Broadway Tower and more fine views. Broadway, that busy, popular, honey-pot of a village, lies below the tower with field paths leading directly to it, thus allowing an opportunity to walk its famous street, sample its tearooms and dodge its traffic before returning to the hills again above Buckland. The continuing route takes you along the scarp edge on a clear track for a while, but on reaching Shenberrow Hill you leave the uplands once more and wander down through lush green meadows to the manicured perfection that is Stanton.

On this initial stage of the walk you will experience the very essence of the Cotswolds, the mellow glory of its buildings and the enchantment of the breezy wolds with their extensive panoramas.

The official start to the walk is by the Market Hall in **Chipping Campden** High Street, but it would be more satisfactory to begin at the Parish Church of St James, which is found at the north-eastern end of the town (grid ref: 155395).

Leaving the church, and the gateway to the long-destroyed Campden House next to it, walk along Church Street passing a row of 17th-century almshouses on your right and a cart wash on the left. On reaching the High Street bear left, pausing as you walk along it to admire the numerous attractive features which make Campden such a delightful place.

The walk begins or ends at the Parish Church of St James, Chipping Campden

33

BUILDINGS OF CHIPPING CAMPDEN

The elegance of Chipping Campden stems from the wool trade, for many of the finest buildings owe their existence directly to it. The open-sided Market Hall, built in 1627, is an eye-catching feature. Nearby is the 14th-century Woolstaplers' Hall, which houses the town's museum; opposite stands Grevel House, dating from 1380. William Grevel, whose home it was, has a large memorial brass in the parish church – reckoned to be one of the best examples of a Cotswold 'wool church'. Next to it stand the fanciful gateway and onion-topped lodges that mark the entrance to one-time Campden House, built by Sir Baptist Hicks for an unbelievable £29,000 in 1615. Thirty years later it was burned down by Royalist troops during the Civil War. Alongside Church Street, on a raised pavement, stands a row of attractive almshouses, also built by Hicks, at a cost of £1000, to house 12 of the local poor. Chipping Campden tourist information: Old Police Station, High Street, Chipping Campden ☎ 01386 841206.

Passing Sheep Street, which breaks away to the left, continue ahead along Lower High Street, but leave this to take the first road on the right by St Catherine's Roman Catholic Church. The road soon bears right, with Birdcage Walk and Hoo Lane branching left by a thatched cottage. Walk along Hoo Lane, and when the surfaced lane ends a farm track continues ahead, rising easily uphill. This is soon accompanied by a footpath, which begins by some barns and eventually brings you to Kincomb Lane. Bear left for about 100 metres, to find a signpost directing you across the road and between fields on an enclosed footpath.

Note that the original metal signposts along the Cotswold Way give distances in kilometres, while the new national trail oak posts are measured in miles.

The path leads to a kissing gate, through which you then turn left along the edge of the escarpment with views extending across the Vale of Evesham – the first of many fine panoramas to be enjoyed along the Cotswold Way. Some seats have been placed here, to make the most of the view, and one of these is found by a topograph marking **Dover's Hill**. From here it is said that on a clear day you can see 60 miles (96km) across the Worcestershire Plain towards Wales. Nearby, in the corner of the meadow by a gate leading into a car park, there's a memorial stone dedicated to Captain Robert Dover.

DOVER'S HILL

Owned by the National Trust, at 755ft (230m) Dover's Hill is one of many fine vantage points along the Cotswold escarpment. It was named after Captain Robert Dover (1582–1652), a wealthy and somewhat eccentric lawyer who organised his first 'Olympick Games' there in 1612. The games included leapfrog, wrestling, skittles and 'shin-kicking', and apart from an interruption during the Civil War, the games continued annually until 1852. Dover's Olympics were revived in 1951, and now take place each spring bank holiday.

Pass through the gate and cross the National Trust car park to a country lane where you bear left, then wander downhill to a small crossroads. Now head to the right, once again following Kingcomb Lane towards Willersey and Broadway. (The left-hand grass verge is the safest place to walk here.) Along this stretch, half-hidden on the right on the edge of Weston Park Wood, is the Kiftsgate Stone, which marks the site of a Saxon meeting place. After about 400 metres leave the lane by way of a stone stile on the left next to a field gate. A few paces later bear right through a gap in a stone wall on the edge of a spinney. This brings you to the Mile Drive.

The Mile Drive is a broad grassy avenue with views now to the left (south-east) into Tilbury Hollow. Halfway along it you cross a farm drive and continue ahead. At the far end go through a gap in a drystone wall on the right, then half-left across a field corner to a second wall. Continue in the same direction until you come to Buckle Street. Across the road the footpath maintains direction to reach a picnic area with a topograph just above the A44 on Fish Hill. At this point you leave Gloucestershire and briefly enter the county of Hereford and Worcester.

Turn left and descend through the picnic site to a car park. Keep ahead to a toilet block where you bear right, go through a gap in a stone wall and cross the A44 with care. Turn right along a tarmac road to pass a quarry, continue beyond a house on a track, and when this ends a footpath takes you into woodland. Emerge to meadowland gruffed with curious humps and hollows, which may be explained by the fact that the site was used as an Anglo-Saxon burial ground – in 1954 a number of human bones were exposed by a mechanical digger.

Soon after bear half-left through a shallow cleave, or dry valley, with **Broadway Tower** seen rising ahead (grid ref: 114362). Shortly before reaching the tower, you will gain a first

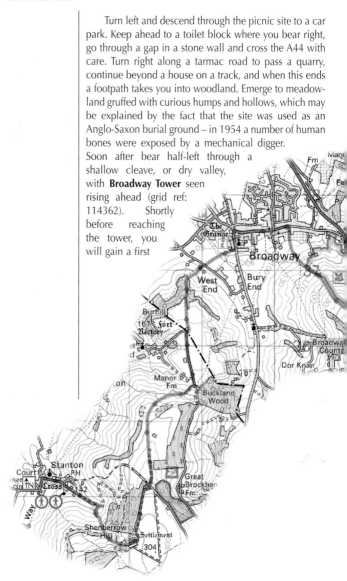

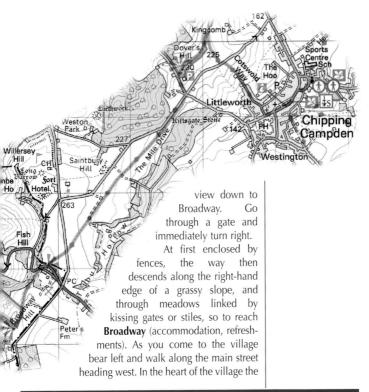

view down to Broadway. Go through a gate and immediately turn right.

At first enclosed by fences, the way then descends along the right-hand edge of a grassy slope, and through meadows linked by kissing gates or stiles, so to reach **Broadway** (accommodation, refreshments). As you come to the village bear left and walk along the main street heading west. In the heart of the village the

BROADWAY TOWER

The top of Broadway Tower is said to be the highest point in the Cotswolds, at 1089ft (332m), although Cleeve Common claims the highest ground. Occupying a grassy knoll, it commands a tremendous panoramic view over the Vale of Evesham, with chequered fields below and the scarp edge folding away in a series of spurs and coombes as far as the eye can see. Designed by James Wyatt in 1798 for the sixth Earl of Coventry, the tower is a Norman-style keep with three rounded turrets. Around it lies part of the Broadway Tower Country Park; the Tower Barn is about 150 years old, while Rookery Barn houses an information centre and restaurant.

The lofty Broadway Tower was built as a landmark folly for the Earl of Coventry.
Standing high above Broadway it commands an impressive view

street is flanked by red-flowering chestnut trees, and lined with shops, tearooms, hotels and houses of mellow stone. On coming to the village green, turn left into Church Street and wander past the Crown and Trumpet and the Parish Church of St Michael and All Angels.

BROADWAY

A quintessential Cotswold village, with a wide street lined with handsome shops, houses and hotels – hence 'broad way'. It is said to have been 'discovered' by William Morris, in whose wake came a number of Victorian artists to extend its fame. The village has a long history, but during the era of the stagecoach it grew in importance, providing accommodation and a change of horses in readiness for the steep haul up Fish Hill. Nowadays horses have been replaced by horsepower, and Broadway is at times a snarl of traffic amid a clutter of commerce. Without traffic the village is a gem: wisteria-clad cottages, 17th-century almshouses, an avenue of red-flowering chestnut trees, a village green and two churches. The oldest of these is St Eadburgh's, which dates from the 12th century, and the other is the Victorian church of St Michael and All Angels, passed on the way out. Tourist information: Cotswold Court, The Green, Broadway ☎01386 852937.

Broadway – mellow stone, wisteria-clad walls, and flower borders

Soon after passing the church turn right onto a track, then go beyond a few houses into the meadowland ahead. The path takes you over a footbridge and across another meadow to West End Lane, across which you have a choice of paths. The right-hand option leads to Buckland, but directly ahead the Cotswold Way goes through a gate and up an enclosed path into a sloping meadow. At the head of the slope enter Broadway Coppice, a woodland mixture of hazel, oak, birch and ash. The path winds on before emerging at a hilltop field. Now bear left along the field edge, and at the end go round the back of a stable-cum-barn, then right to join a track heading left. At this point you re-enter Gloucestershire.

The farm track takes you almost due south towards more wooded hills, before entering an untidy farmyard area. Bear right to follow a rough track going along the right-hand edge of a field, rising steadily and with tree-screened views soon showing into the valley off to your right, with Buckland nestling at the foot of the slope.

Continue on the track, passing through a field gate with a crown of trees half-left ahead, and walk below a lovely line of beeches to gain the crest of a ridge. Views open once more. To the left stands a handsome farm and a few barns. The ridge narrows considerably, green and rabbit-shorn, with grey drystone walls criss-crossing, the slopes bearing a mixture of scrub and grassland habitats. ◄

The track takes you past a region of hollows on the left; these are one-time quarries. About 200 metres later, immediately after a junction of tracks, bear right over a cattlegrid and walk along a cart track which curves through a long meadowland, keeping near the scarp edge with the mixed woods of Long Hill Plantation on your right.

Coming to Shenberrow Hill ◄ (grid ref: 080335) pass to the right of a farm, go through a field gate and descend to the right through a tight cleave (or dry valley) among trees. Be warned that this 'dry valley' can be rather muddy in inclement weather. At the bottom of the cleave veer left, cross a stile, then descend along the right-hand side of meadowland. Before long bear right

In their season cowslips and early purple orchids paint the hillside with a flush of colour. Bullfinch and yellow hammer flit to and fro while jackdaws circle lazily over the topmost woods.

Shenberrow Hill above Stanton is the site of an Iron Age hill fort of about 2½ acres (1 hectare). When it was excavated in 1935, various artefacts were revealed, among them pieces of pottery, a bronze bracelet and two bone needles.

over a stile into an adjacent meadow and continue downhill towards a pond seen in a hollow. This is Stanton Reservoir, a pleasant corner giving a dazzle of light amidst the trees. Keep above the pond to the right, go through a gate and bear left to pass below its northern end. A track now leads down to **Stanton** (accommodation, refreshments), a glorious little village with almost-perfect cottages lining an almost-perfect street (grid ref: 070342). ▶

Note For refreshments at the Mount Inn, turn right along the village street – the Cotswold Way turns left.

STANTON

It has been called the perfect Cotswold village, and not without good reason. It is, in truth, almost too perfect, like a Hollywood director's idea of a 'quaint' English village. In these days of bland architecture, insensitive development and myopic planning, Stanton very nearly jars with a sense of unreality! Its origins are simple. The village was basically a group of 16th-century cottages and farmhouses (Stanton, or Stan Tun, means 'stony farm') built from local stone in such a sympathetic manner that they seem to have grown straight out of the ground. When Sir Philip Stott came to Stanton Court in 1906 he found the village rather neglected, and from then until his death in 1937 he spent much money and architectural talent on restoring it to the splendour we see today. Unlike Broadway, Stanton has not been over-run by the motor car, or by advertisements. As such one wanders through in a dream of past centuries.

Stanton High Street is lined with attractive houses

SECTION 2

Stanton to Winchcombe

Distance	8 miles (12½km)
Maps	Harvey's Cotswold Way 1:40,000
	OS Landranger 150 Worcester, The Malverns &
	Surrounding Area 1:50,000
	OS Explorer OL45 The Cotswolds 1:25,000
Accommodation	Stanway, Wood Stanway, Hailes and Winchcombe
Refreshments	Hailes and Winchcombe

A series of field paths leads the continuing way out of Stanton to Stanway, then along the foot of the slope to reach Wood Stanway from where a steep ascent is made to Stumps Cross. The only real climb on this part of the walk, it's followed by an easy track (the ancient Campden Lane) to Beckbury Camp and Cromwell's Clump, from where it is said Thomas Cromwell watched as Hailes Abbey was dismantled. Field paths take you to a narrow lane that leads beside orchards to the remains of Hailes Abbey (worth a visit), then across more fields to Winchcombe.

Apart from the steep climb above Wood Stanway, this is an easy, gentle stage. It wanders through peaceful countryside with soft views to enjoy, not only from the scarp edge, but also from the foot of the slope, where you gaze off to isolated hills (outliers) such as Alderton Hill near Toddington, and Oxenton Hill north-west of Winchcombe.

On entering the village street in Stanton, turn left and wander between honey-coloured cottages (note the medieval village cross halfway through), and bear left where the road forks shortly after passing the church. When it curves to the right, go straight ahead on a farm drive, and after about 80 metres pass a red, corrugated-iron Dutch barn, then bear right through a gate. The continuing footpath skirts the base of the hills, while off to your right spread the lowlands of the Vale of Evesham,

broken here and there by groups of individual hills and distant green ridges topped by woodlands, a soft, gentle landscape to admire.

The Cotswold Way enters Stanway through Stanway Park

This is a fine, easy stretch of the walk, the path leading alongside meadows and finally bringing you to the parkland of Stanway House, where long avenues of stately oaks and chestnut trees throw welcome shade on a hot summer's day. Across the parkland, guided by oak marker posts, come to a country lane (note the thatched cricket pavilion perched on staddle stones opposite). Bear left and walk into the hamlet of **Stanway** (accommodation), noting on the way the huge tithe barn in the ground of Stanway House behind the church.

STANWAY

Church Stanway as it is also known, is even smaller than Stanton – a clutch of buildings in the shadow, so to speak, of the Jacobean manor, Stanway House. The village has an air of feudalism about it – the church, the houses, even the trees, appear to come under manorial patronage. In almost 1300 years' ownership the manor has changed hands only once (except by inheritance), so perhaps it is not surprising that the community should appear so closely knit. As well as the manor and 12th-century Church of St Peter (with much Victorian reconstruction), note the massive tithe barn, the three-storey Jacobean gatehouse with gables adorned with scallop-shell finials, and the 13th-century watermill that once belonged to the abbots of Tewkesbury.

The Jacobean gatehouse of Stanway House stands next to the church

The lane winds in front of the church and past the fanciful south gatehouse of Stanway House (grid ref: 061323). A few paces beyond this you leave the lane by a large yew tree and turn left. A narrow footpath takes you left of a blacksmith's workshop and the remains of a watermill, crosses a small meadow and brings you onto the B4077. Go left for about 40 metres, then head to the right on a continuation of the Cotswold Way along a path enclosed by a hedge and a fence containing a plantation.

This path soon entices across low-lying fields towards the hamlet of Wood Stanway. (Stanway, which you have just left, is sometimes known as Church Stanway to avoid confusion.) Behind and above the hamlet runs the Cotswold skyline on which you can see a line of individual trees. The route eventually angles up to the left-hand end of these.

On coming to Wood Stanway (accommodation), a community still, it appears, committed to working the land, head to the left along a narrow road which soon rises past Glebe Farm, then continues as a farm track. Above the farm the path winds up through meadows sloping the hillside, keeping to the left of a line of power cables. Although the path is not always evident on the ground, there are waymarks to guide you.

45

Pass well to the right of a house called Lower Coscombe, then bear left above it and follow the waymarks leading on a diagonal ascent of the hill. There is a narrow line of a path which brings you to the head of the slope at the left-hand end of the row of trees seen earlier – a memorial seat has been placed here to exploit the wonderful view. Keep to the left of a drystone wall and follow it to the road junction at Stumps Cross (grid ref: 076304).

Bear right immediately round the wall and onto the farm track of Campden Lane, a one-time sheep drove-road, which is now followed for about ½ mile (800m). Before long you will pass a cluster of farm buildings on the right, among which there is a corrugated-iron shed on staddle stones.

Continue along the track until it brings you to a small wood with a gate. Do not go through this gate, but instead turn right onto a path striking north-west along-side the wood by a drystone wall. Pass through a gap in the wall and resume direction, now with a large field on your left. In the bottom corner bear left, still skirting the field boundary (big views into the Vale of Evesham again). Maintaining direction you will come to the hill fort of **Beckbury Camp** and the clump of beech trees marking the spot where Thomas Cromwell is said to have overlooked the dismantling of Hailes Abbey.

BECKBURY CAMP

To the east of Hailes Abbey is Beckbury Camp, the site of an Iron Age hill fort of more than 4 acres (1½ hectares). It originally consisted of a single ditch and rampart, but the ditch has since been filled, although along the east side of the rampart its position can still be identified. Located on the scarp edge the hill fort would have been comparatively easy to defend.

Go through the gate, bear right and descend among the beeches, then below the trees veer left to cross a large meadowland. With the guidance of waymarks make a gentle diagonal descent through a series of meadows linked by gates to reach an enclosed crossing track. A signpost here gives directions. Turn right and walk downhill along the track among trees, with orchards on the left and Hailes Wood to your right. When the track brings you onto a lane, note that refreshments are available at Hayles Fruit Farm, which has a tearoom and farm shop (to gain this, turn left).

Continue down the lane and you will shortly come to **Hailes Abbey**. A few paces beyond the abbey remains, and just before the little Norman church, bear left through a kissing gate and into a meadow. Hailes Abbey ruins can be seen over the fence on the left. The meadow footpath brings you to a collection of cottages, then onto a lane where you turn right. This is Salter's Lane, an old saltway and part of a major route from Droitwich Spa to the Thames Valley which crosses the Cotswolds between Hailes and Lechlade.

HAILES ABBEY

Now managed and maintained by English Heritage, Hailes Abbey was built by Richard, Earl of Cornwall and brother of Henry III, as a thanksgiving for having survived a near-shipwreck. The abbey was consecrated in 1251 for a community of Cistercian monks, and when a phial purporting to contain the blood of Christ was presented by Richard's second son, Edmund, in 1270, Hailes became a place of pilgrimage for nearly 300 years. But in 1538 the phial was taken for analysis to London where the contents were pronounced as nothing more than 'honey clarified and coloured with saffron'. The following year, during the dissolution of the monasteries, the abbey was closed, its ornaments taken away, and the buildings sold to a private dealer in 1542. Now only the ivy-clad archways, crumbling masonry and clearly defined foundations remain. Nearby, on the opposite side of the lane, stands the 12th-century Church of St Nicholas, where a number of medieval wall paintings make the building worthy of a visit.

About 100 metres along Salter's Lane bear left onto a track. As this begins to rise up the hillside, keep alert for a footpath breaking away to the right by a pair of oak trees. Follow this path along the edge of a field, then

Skeletal ruins of Hailes Abbey can be seen from the Cotswold Way

strike away half-left to the far corner where a waymark can be seen. Go over a stile in the hedge, bear left round the edge of a field for a few yards, then pass through a metal kissing gate into the next meadow. There is no real footpath to be seen on the ground, but you simply head diagonally across two meadows linked by gates and a footbridge, with brief views of Winchcombe ahead. You will come to a stile giving onto a track which leads to the outskirts of Winchcombe. The track becomes a narrow metalled road – Puck Pit Lane – bordered by neat, trimmed hedges. On reaching the B4632, turn left and walk into **Winchcombe**, a pleasant small town with a range of accommodation, pubs, restaurants, shops, a post office, and so on.

WINCHCOMBE

The largest community so far met on the Cotswold Way, Winchcombe is still only a small town whose main street is adorned with many archetypal Cotswold buildings in typical Cotswold stone, although without the overall uniformity and grace exhibited in such places as Campden, Broadway or Stanton. Once an important settlement, Winchcombe was the capital of a Saxon shire and seat of Mercian royalty. Offa, King of Mercia, dedicated a nunnery here in AD790 and an abbey was established by his successor, Kenulf, in AD811. Kenulf had a son, Kenelm, who was murdered at the behest of his ambitious sister, and as a consequence of Kenelm's death assorted miracles were attributed to him which, in turn, made Winchcombe a place of pilgrimage. The abbey has gone, but the Parish Church of St Peter, built in the 15th century, owes something to abbey money, which helped to pay for it. Among its more notable features are the 40 gargoyles that adorn the outer walls at gutter level. Elsewhere in the town you will find a pair of wooden stocks outside the Folk Museum, and among its buildings are two or three fine old inns, and Tudor houses and cottages with roses growing at their porches. Seen from the continuing route is Sudeley Castle, details of which are given under Section 3. The way out of town is by way of attractive Vineyard Street, formerly known as Duck Street, after the ducking stool in the River Isbourne. Tourist information: Town Hall, High Street, Winchcombe ☎ 01242 602925.

SECTION 3

Winchcombe to Cleeve Hill

Distance	6½ miles (10½km)
Maps	Harvey's Cotswold Way 1:40,000
	OS Landranger 163 Cheltenham & Cirencester
	Area 1:50,000
	OS Explorer OL45 The Cotswolds, and 179 Gloucester,
	Cheltenham & Stroud 1:25,000
Accommodation	Cleeve Hill and Bishop's Cleeve (+1½ miles (2½km))
Refreshments	None until Cleeve Hill (just off the route)

On this short, but rather strenuous, section of the walk, a fair amount of height has to be gained. It's both a scenic and historically interesting stretch, beginning shortly after leaving Winchcombe with magnificent Studeley Castle seen across the fields, then passing near the tree-enclosed site of a Roman villa, before the walk leads steeply uphill to discover Belas Knap, the first of the great Neolithic burial chambers of the route. The way then treads a wide expanse of country *en route* to Cleeve Common, a vast, moorland-like area of unenclosed land. On its tour round the common the way makes a long 4 mile (6½km) loop (not all of it on this section), whereas a few hundred yards on paths and tracks heading west would bring you onto the continuing route! Such is the nature of long-distance walking. However, visual gains are substantial, for splendid panoramas are a just reward for following the waymarked path. Cleeve Common is above the 1000ft (305m) contour, while lying just below it on the northern slope is the small village of Cleeve Hill, where bed-and-breakfast accommodation can be found.

Having entered Winchcombe along the B4632, follow the road into the centre of town but, shortly before reaching the parish church, turn left into Vineyard Street (signed to **Sudeley Castle**). Immediately after the road crosses the River Isbourne go through a kissing gate on

the right and walk ahead across a meadow to a second kissing gate at the far corner. With a hedgerow on your right maintain direction with Winchcombe seen through gaps in the hedge, and eventually come onto Corndean Lane. Bear left along the lane for about 400 metres.

Vineyard Street in Winchcombe leads down to the River Isbourne

SUDELEY CASTLE

The present Sudeley Castle dates from the 15th century, but this is a re-building by Ralph Boteler of an earlier 12th-century castle. Boteler, who became lord chancellor and was made Baron Sudeley, created a magnificent building, but he backed the wrong side in the Wars of the Roses and his property was confiscated by Edward IV. The castle eventually passed into the hands of Henry VIII, after whose death his widow, Katherine Parr, married Lord Seymour and came to live here. Shortly after giving birth to a daughter, Mary, in 1548, Katherine died and was buried in a lead coffin in St Mary's Chapel. Today the remains of the Elizabethan banqueting hall, the tithe barn, Portmore Tower and St Mary's Chapel all survive and date from Boteler's time. The castle and grounds are open to the public.

Shortly before it curves to the left, enter a drive on the right where a sign gives 1½ miles to Belas Knap.

Walking up this drive the outer edge of Cleeve Common can be seen above to the southwest. Pass a cricket pitch on the right, soon after which the drive curves. Here you go through a kissing gate and walk up a sloping meadow towards woodland, on the way gaining a splendid view left to Sudeley Castle. At the head of the slope come onto a junction of lanes at grid ref: 019263. Walk up the lane ahead (sign to Belas Knap) for a very short distance to a signed path on the right opposite a lay-by. This lay-by is about 400 metres from the site of **Wadfield Roman Villa** – not open to the public.

The path rises through woods, and when you emerge from them, bear left along the lower edge of another sloping meadow. On coming to a corner turn right and walk up the slope, through a kissing gate at the top and continue along the left-hand boundary of a hilltop field, alongside more woodland and into an enclosure containing **Belas Knap**, a Neolithic

WADFIELD ROMAN VILLA

Situated above Winchcombe and hidden from the Cotswold Way by a screen of conifers, Wadfield Roman Villa is one of several Roman buildings in the district. The site was excavated in 1894–5, having been discovered 30 years previously by a farm worker while ploughing. Occupying an exposed hillside overlooking the north-east, the villa consisted of a courtyard, at least two heated rooms, and two others with mosaic pavements. A shed on the site contains sections of floor mosaic.

burial chamber and one of the finest historic sites of the whole walk. An information board gives details (grid ref: 021255).

Having entered the walled enclosure, allow due time to study the barrow, then leave it and head a little south of west along the right-hand boundary of a large field, following the line of a dry-stone wall. At the end of the field continue on a farm track until it dips into a hollow at Wontley Farm, where another track breaks away to the right by a barn. This is the route to follow. It rises through more large open fields and passes beneath a line of high-voltage power cables.

Eventually the track takes you through a gate and then offers several path options. Take the right branch ahead, which leads over a rough, moorland-like area brightened with much gorse. This is the start of **Cleeve Common,** the highest land on the Cotswold Way. Ahead you will notice three tall transmitter towers which will appear and disappear with annoying frequency throughout the long loop of the common. ▸

Many tracks criss-cross the common, but at all junctions there are distinctive marker posts to guide you, the

Note Soon after joining Cleeve Common it would be possible to break away south-west-ward on a series of tracks and paths south of the towers to rejoin the way above Prestbury, thus shortcutting the route, but missing some of the loveliest views. In emergencies, however, this short cut could be a useful exit from the exposed common.

BELAS KNAP

A fine example of the chambered tombs, or long barrows, of the Severn-Cotswold Group. The name means hilltop beacon, which suggests the site was used by the Saxons, for it stands above Winchcombe, which was occupied during Saxon times. Belas Knap, a wedge-shaped mound measuring some 178ft (54m) long, 60ft (18m) wide and about 13ft (4m) at its highest point, dates from about 3000BC. At its northern end is a false portal with two horns lined with drystone walling and blocked by a massive slab. When it was excavated in 1863, the remains of five children and the skull of an adult were discovered behind the portal. There are two chambers along the eastern side, one on the west and another at the southern end, reached by shallow passages walled with stones laid in almost identical fashion to many of the drystone walls seen along the Cotswold Way. No less than 26 burials were found to have been made in the paired north-east and north-west chambers, and the remains of two males and two females in the south-eastern chamber. The 1863 excavation also revealed Roman coins and pottery.

direction to maintain being roughly north-west. On coming to a steep and narrow cleave, you descend to the Washpool, a small pond probably used as a sheep-dip. Passing alongside it, the way then curves round the foot of the hills keeping left of a wall-enclosed woodland.

The path forks, with one branch heading right over a stile into the walled Postlip enclosure. Do not cross this, but instead bear left to find a waymark post directing a narrow path steeply up the hillside. As a consolation for the effort involved in climbing this slope, fine views are to be had off to the right.

Waymarks lead you on and across the fairways of a golf course, with the village of **Cleeve Hill** coming into view below. Should you require either refreshment or accommodation, follow signs directing you to the clubhouse. Beyond this a road leads directly into Cleeve Hill, which has accommodation and refreshments (grid ref: 984268), while the much larger Bishop's Cleeve lies just below. This too has accommodation, including (at present) camping facilities.

CLEEVE COMMON

Cleeve Common contains the highest land on the Cotswolds escarpment at 1083ft (330m). The last expanse of unenclosed land in the region, it covers an area of about 3 sq miles (7½ sq km) and is designated a grade 1 site of special scientific interest, with various orchids, glow-worms, and many different types of butterfly attracted by its range of habitats. In spite of the common's popularity with walkers and golfing enthusiasts, there are large areas that seem as remote as almost anywhere in Britain. Because of its height, this large upland plateau is often swept by mists, when it can be a bleak and mysterious place. But in good conditions the vast panoramic views revealed are among the finest anywhere along the Cotswold Way. The Malvern Hills and Brecon Beacons are among the distant features.

CLEEVE HILL

A very small village that seems to hang from the steep north-west slope of Cleeve Common, with notable views over the plain below. Several Iron Age earthworks above the village tell of long-past settlements. One, known as the Ring, covers about ½ acre (¼ hectare), and within it there is what may have been a hut platform. On Cleeve Common, Cleeve Hill Municipal Golf Course is owned by Tewkesbury Borough Council.

SECTION 4

Cleve Hill to Dowdeswell (A40)

Distance	6 miles (9½km)
Maps	Harvey's Cotswold Way 1:40,000
	OS Landranger 163 Cheltenham & Cirencester Area 1:50,000
	OS Explorer 179 Gloucester, Cheltenham & Stroud 1:25,000
Accommodation	Dowdeswell
Refreshments	Dowdeswell

This is another short but splendid stage with a number of outstanding views. There will be a small amount of road walking, but this is limited to a country lane with little, if any, traffic to spoil the peace of the countryside. Mostly the way follows the western edge of the Cotswold escarpment high above Cheltenham. Some of it goes through a butterfly reserve, some is in woodland, some goes through an agricultural landscape and part of the route is on ragged heath. It begins by heading south along the scarp edge of Cleeve Common, but when at last this has been deserted you cross a seemingly remote patch of farmland before descending along a line of woods to Dowdeswell Reservoir and the A40 Cheltenham-to-Oxford road. At the time of writing accommodation was available at the end of this stage.

If coming from Cleeve Hill village, return to the golf course on Cleeve Common and follow signs (right) south-west of the clubhouse on a traverse of the hillside. A good track with Cotswold Way marker posts is your guide, from which there are views down to the sprawl of Bishop's Cleeve at the foot of the slope. Before long waymarks direct you away from the track, and up to a trig point vantage point at 1040ft (317m) where there's also a topograph showing points of interest in the long views which stretch to the Brecon Beacons and Malvern Hills. Bear

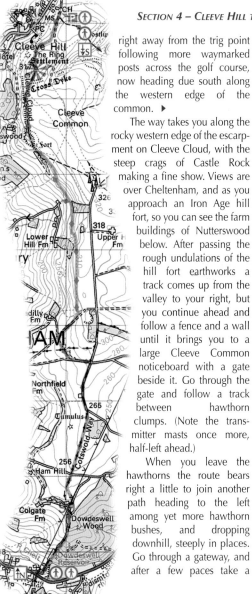

right away from the trig point following more waymarked posts across the golf course, now heading due south along the western edge of the common. ▶

The way takes you along the rocky western edge of the escarpment on Cleeve Cloud, with the steep crags of Castle Rock making a fine show. Views are over Cheltenham, and as you approach an Iron Age hill fort, so you can see the farm buildings of Nutterswood below. After passing the rough undulations of the hill fort earthworks a track comes up from the valley to your right, but you continue ahead and follow a fence and a wall until it brings you to a large Cleeve Common noticeboard with a gate beside it. Go through the gate and follow a track between hawthorn clumps. (Note the transmitter masts once more, half-left ahead.)

When you leave the hawthorns the route bears right a little to join another path heading to the left among yet more hawthorn bushes, and dropping downhill, steeply in places. Go through a gateway, and after a few paces take a

It is almost impossible to give precise directions because of the number of paths and golf course trails, but Cotswold Way marker posts are maintained in good order and are your best guide.

57

Making a traverse of Cleeve Common, Castle Rock can be seen on the scarp edge

narrow path left alongside a nature-reserve boundary fence. The path divides. Take the right branch curving along the lower edge of a beech wood. When the wood ends go through a gate into the Bill Smyllie Reserve (in the care of the organisation 'Butterfly Conservation'). Maintain direction on a path which eventually curves left, then forks. Take the right branch.

Coming out of a section enclosed by bushes, cross an open area and leave the butterfly reserve over a stile. The way now continues between gorse bushes. Coming to a four-way crossing, turn right and slope downhill a little, still among gorse, then reach a major crossing path. Bear left uphill for a few paces to reach a pole supporting overhead cables, where a waymark directs you to the right onto a sunken track sloping gently downhill, with a disused quarry on your left.

The track brings you to a gate at the top of a narrow, surfaced lane. Go through the gate and branch left on a footpath aiming alongside woods with a large meadow-land stretching away to your right. At this point fine views show across the valley to the continuing Cotswold escarpment.

At the end of the woods bear left along a narrow country lane through an avenue of splendid beech trees.

At a minor crossroads turn right. This lane also has a row of ancient pollarded beech trees alongside it. When it curves sharply leftwards leave the lane and continue straight ahead through a kissing gate, then along an enclosed track with a drystone wall on your right. ▷ When the wall ends the track continues ahead, leading to a very narrow lane (grid ref: 991211).

Over the wall there are views to enjoy of the distant Black Mountains.

Across the lane go through a kissing gate and walk ahead along the right-hand edge of a field. Halfway down, a waymark directs you half-left across the field to another kissing gate about 30 metres left of barns at Colgate Farm. Cross the farm drive, through yet another kissing gate, and onto an enclosed path among trees. This narrow footpath leads alongside Dowdeswell Wood Nature Reserve – full of colour in springtime with an abundance of bluebells and white-starred ramsons (wild garlic) forming vast carpets among the trees. The path is very steep in places, and greasy in wet weather, when you will need to exercise caution, but a number of steps have been cut into the slope to ease the gradient.

Near the foot of the slope **Dowdeswell Reservoir** may be seen to the left (grid ref: 987197). At the time of writing, a cottage on the right (Langett) offers refreshments and accommodation for Cotswold Way walkers (see *The Cotswold Way Handbook & Accommodation List* for up-to-date information). Beyond the cottage cross a sluice and follow a stony drive. Shortly after this curves to the right, go through a gate on the left and climb a slope to the A40. Cross the road with care to the left of The Reservoir Inn.

DOWDESWELL RESERVOIR

Dowdeswell Reservoir was created in the late 19th century by damming the River Chelt, upstream of Charlton Kings, in order to supply the needs of the fast-growing town of Cheltenham. Despite its close proximity to the Cotswold Way, it is barely glimpsed by passing walkers.

SECTION 5

Dowdeswell (A40) to Birdlip

Distance	9½ miles (15km)
Maps	Harvey's Cotswold Way 1:40,000
	OS Landranger 163 Cheltenham & Cirencester Area 1:50,000
	OS Explorer 179 Gloucester, Cheltenham & Stroud 1:25,000
Accommodation	Charlton Kings (+ ½ mile (800m)), Little Witcombe (+1½ miles (2½km)) and Birdlip
Refreshments	Seven Springs, Crickley Hill and Birdlip

Away from the A40 the Cotswold Way enters woodland before angling up onto the scarp edge once more. Here the route has been much improved, thanks to national trail status. In the past you had a choice of either following the busy A436, or making a detour through further woodland and across fields on the way to Seven Springs, but now the scarp edge is enjoyed a little longer before a new path leads to the Seven Springs crossroads. From here the way makes a north-westerly curve to regain the scarp edge, where once again there are magnificent views to enjoy. Along Charlton Kings Common, past the stubby finger of the Devil's Chimney below Leckhampton Hill, the route takes you on to Crickley Hill Country Park and its fascinating archaeological site. From there a final 2 miles (3km) of scarp and woodland bring you to Birdlip and the end of this stage.

Having crossed the A40 near The Reservoir Inn follow a footpath winding just below the road, then curve right on a track leading into Lineover Wood, which is owned by the Woodland Trust. Slant up the left-hand side of the trees before entering the woods proper. Mostly surfaced with stone chippings, the path rises steadily, then mounts a series of wood-braced steps. Emerging into a meadow, continue up its left-hand boundary to the top corner.

Lineover Wood, seen from near Old Dole Farm

Through a kissing gate bear right round the corner of the next field, and via another gate enter an upper section of Lineover Wood, the successor to a forest mentioned in documents as being here as long ago as the ninth century.

The delightful woodland path makes a steady descending traverse of the slope amid a riot of birdsong, and finally emerges near Old Dole Farm (with a small reservoir below it). Go up the sloping meadow beneath power cables to the top corner where a gate will be found among a group of trees. Through the gate bear right to skirt the lower edge of a steep hillside meadow, but soon break away left onto a narrow path climbing diagonally up to the wood-crowned crest of Wistley Hill. ▶

Turn right alongside Wistley Plantation, where the path keeps to the edge of the escarpment, and continue when the wood ends, now curving slightly left. About 200 metres from the woodland go through a gate on the left, then turn right on an enclosed path which takes you round two sides of a large field, then into Wistley Grove. At a crossing track turn right and descend to a gate beside the A436. Here you cross a private road, then go through a gate into a field where you walk along its left headland.

There's a welcome seat at the top of this ascent where you can collapse, catch your breath, and enjoy a panoramic view that includes Cleeve Common to the north.

61

SEVEN SPRINGS

Seven Springs is often claimed to be the source of the River Thames, although this is a moot point, since it is the River Churn which begins here, and that is only a tributary of the Thames. The springs leak from the water table beneath Hartley Hill and may be found a short distance down the A436 in a tree-clad hollow north of the road.

Note For refreshments, the Seven Springs Inn is found a short distance ahead alongside the A436.

This eventually brings you to the A435, a few paces north of the **Seven Springs** crossroads (grid ref: 968172). ◄

Cross the road with caution to a Cotswold Way sign which directs you to

the right along a minor road, soon passing a wind-pump in the left-hand field. When the road curves left keep straight ahead on an enclosed footpath, but at a junction you bear left and follow the left-hand boundary of an enclosed rectangular meadow rich in wild flowers in springtime. Enter a spinney, then out again along the scarp edge. To your right the transmitter towers on Cleeve Common can be seen once more, with Cheltenham below.

This is a fine stretch with splendid views overlooking the Severn Vale. The path rises along the scarp edge of Charlton Kings Common to Hartley Hill and, among gorse bushes with numerous hollows where ragstone has been extracted for drystone walling, onto the flat-topped Leckhampton Hill with its trig point and more fine views.

Continue along the scarp edge and, a short distance beyond a topograph, a sign on the right offers a short diversion to see the **Devil's Chimney**, a noted pinnacle of rock projecting from the lower shelf of the scarp face (grid ref: 946184).

The Cotswold Way continues its scarp-edge path before descending to a narrow country lane where you turn left and walk uphill. Near the crown of the hill bear right on a bridleway track which slips along the right-hand side of a field,

DEVIL'S CHIMNEY

One of the major landmarks of the walk, the Devil's Chimney is a craggy finger of rock projecting from the scarp face terrace below Leckhampton Hill. Throughout the 18th century extensive quarrying took place here, and the exposed pinnacle is a result of this industry. Local quarrymen apparently trimmed the chimney as part of a hoax. In more recent times repair work was instigated to arrest the effects of erosion, which threatened the landmark with collapse. Although climbing the pinnacle is now prohibited, for many years it made a popular scramble, and the record stands at 13 people on the top at one time!

passes a few secluded houses, goes through woodland, then narrows on its way to a minor road. Turn right and, passing Ullenwood Manor on your left, come to cross-roads. Cross directly ahead into Greenway Lane, another of the Cotswold drove-roads which runs straight as a die between neat hedges and drystone walls. If you gaze over your right shoulder you will see the steep cut of the scarp edge and the Devil's Chimney· standing clear. Along Greenway Lane you pass a former army camp, now used by Gloucestershire Fire and Rescue Service as a fire-fighter training unit, and soon after come to a beech grove with Shurdington Long Barrow in the field before it. When the lane bears slightly left, leave it to go up some steps on the left onto a continuing path alongside the wood. Once again the way edges the scarp slope with yet more lovely views to the west.

The path leads through a narrow strip of beech woods, which help frame the views and diffuse the light into slanting pillars, then you come to **Crickley Hill** Country Park, with its hill fort, complete with observation platform built to ease problems of erosion where excavations have taken place. Views from here include the Black Mountains, Forest of Dean and the Malvern Hills. (There are public toilets and a visitor centre in the car park.)

CRICKLEY HILL

Crickley Hill is one of the Cotswolds' great archaeological discoveries. Some time between 4000 and 3000BC, in the Neolithic period, more than 3 acres (1/ hectares) of the hill were occupied as a camp, consisting of a single ditch and a bank. A second occupation took place about 700BC by Iron Age settlers, when 9 acres (3½ hectares) were used for housing, for the storage of crops, and as livestock pens. A rampart and palisaded walkway surrounded the camp, and a 6ft (1.8m) ditch was dug. A third camp was made here following a period when Crickley Hill had been abandoned by these first Iron Age settlers, and during this final occupation round houses were built. This term of settlement ended with destruction by fire. On the observation platform a series of information panels describe the various stages of occupation.

From the observation platform continue ahead to the end of a promontory by a drystone wall, where there are more beautiful views. Turn left, go through a gate and follow the wall, beyond which the slope plunges abruptly to a few houses. Keep beside the wall, then go ahead into beech woods. Waymarks eventually bring you out near a very busy roundabout at the Air Balloon pub (grid ref: 935161).

Cross with great care and pass along the left-hand side of the pub beside the A417. Just beyond a bus shelter and a telephone kiosk, the pavement dips and a narrow, waymarked path heads away to the right among trees to bring you onto the scarp edge once more. The path leads on a switchback course along Barrow Wake, enjoying broad panoramas which include the Vale of Gloucester, May Hill, the Black Mountains and Brecon Beacons beyond, and the curving line of the wolds ahead. ▶

A fence accompanies the path to a field, and across this you enter woodland. Bear right. On coming to a junction of paths continue ahead for a further 70 metres to a promontory descriptively known as the Peak, where lovely secluded views are to be had. (Originally the Cotswold Way climbed the steep path below the Peak, but was re-routed from Crickley Hill.)

Backtrack from the Peak to the path junction and take the right-hand branch winding among trees and onto a woodland track. This leads directly to the road immediately below the village of **Birdlip,** where accommodation and refreshments can be found. To reach the village walk uphill for about 400 metres. To continue the walk, cross the road to where the path descends among trees.

It was here, along Barrow Wake, that in the 19th century a quarryman exposed a female burial site containing a silver brooch, bronze owls, a decorated bucket and a richly ornamented bronze mirror. These finds are to be seen in the Gloucester City Museum.

BIRDLIP

Birdlip stands on the edge of the escarpment on the course of the Roman Ermin Street (also sometimes called Ermin Way), which ran from Gloucester (Glevum) to Cirencester (Corinium), and which is not to be confused with the similarly named Ermine Street (or Way), which runs from London to Lincoln.

SECTION 6

Birdlip to Painswick

Distance	7 miles (11km)
Maps	Harvey's Cotswold Way 1:40,000
	OS Landranger 163 Cheltenham & Cirencester Area,
	and 162 Gloucester & Forest of Dean Area 1:50,000
	OS Explorer 179 Gloucester, Cheltenham &
	Stroud 1:25,000
Accommodation	Cooper's Hill and Painswick
Refreshments	Cooper's Hill, Prinknash and Painswick

This is another lovely walk, much of it through woodland, but with panoramic viewpoints to enjoy too, such as that from the head of the cheese-rolling slope at Cooper's Hill, and also from the hill fort on Painswick Beacon. Painswick itself is another of the gems of the Cotswolds, an old market town built of the whitest of all local stones, famed for its clipped churchyard yews and table tombs, but with much more to admire in its maze of backstreets.

The way leaves Birdlip Hill and takes to woods immediately, cutting round the northern scarp slope with intimate vistas through the trees, then up steeply onto Cooper's Hill. More woodlands continue the walk on a south-westerly course to pass above Prinknash Abbey. You then cross the A46 at Cranham Corner and head out to the common land and manicured fairways of a golf course below Painswick Beacon, before catching sight of the hamlet of Paradise on the final downhill walk to Painswick.

The continuing path heads south from the road which descends Birdlip Hill and is found directly opposite the woodland track leading from the Peak. The path slopes downhill among trees and undergrowth with views into the valley where Brockworth lies in a sprawl beyond Witcombe Reservoir. On coming to a crossing path, head to the left, with acres of fields and meadows on the right

sweeping towards that reservoir. The path forks and you bear left, rising easily through Witcombe Wood. At a broad cross-track bear right, and at the next crossing go straight ahead.

Below Birdlip, Witcombe Reservoir can be seen from Witcombe Wood

There are numerous paths and trackways in the beech woods as you curve round the 'combe' of Witcombe, but confusion is avoided by generous, yet not overly intrusive, waymarking. On occasion the correct route deserts a broad track for what seems a minor path, so remain alert for signs. If the onward route is not obvious at any stage, simply look for a guiding CW arrow. At one point you pass the stone pillars of a gateway to Witcombe Park Estate.

▶ Some of the route follows a bridleway and, as is common along such tracks, this can be rather muddy when churned by horses' hooves. Fallow deer roam these woodlands and lone walkers stepping lightly may be rewarded by a sighting. Often, as the route leads along the woodland edge, fine views are given out across the reservoir to a curve of folding hills and meadows, while in the coombe to the right, near Cooper's Hill Farm, is the site of **Witcombe Roman Villa**.

As with many other woodland stretches on the long walk from Chipping Campden to Bath, this one is especially attractive in springtime, with vast carpets of bluebells, wood anemones and ramsons.

67

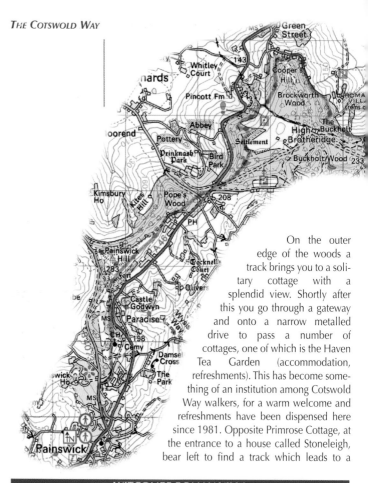

On the outer edge of the woods a track brings you to a solitary cottage with a splendid view. Shortly after this you go through a gateway and onto a narrow metalled drive to pass a number of cottages, one of which is the Haven Tea Garden (accommodation, refreshments). This has become something of an institution among Cotswold Way walkers, for a warm welcome and refreshments have been dispensed here since 1981. Opposite Primrose Cottage, at the entrance to a house called Stoneleigh, bear left to find a track which leads to a

WITCOMBE ROMAN VILLA

The Roman villa stands on the spring-line near the foot of the northern slopes between Birdlip Hill and Cooper's Hill. Dating from the first century AD the villa was built on land first exploited by Iron Age man, and excavations have unearthed sections of a bath house with fine mosaics depicting seascapes as well as fish. The villa is in the care of English Heritage.

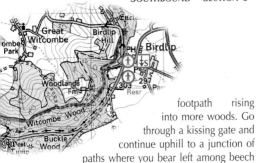

footpath rising into more woods. Go through a kissing gate and continue uphill to a junction of paths where you bear left among beech trees and eventually gain the open glade of **Cooper's Hill**, on which there's a maypole (grid ref: 892146). Glorious views are to be had over Brockworth and Gloucester, the distant curve of the Cotswold escarpment and, far off, the Malvern Hills. It is claimed that the Black Mountains can also be seen from here.

COOPER'S HILL

Cooper's Hill is noted not just as a superb viewpoint, but also for the annual festival of cheese-rolling, which takes place on its excessively steep grass slope. The origins and antiquity of this ritual are unknown, but the festivities are now held on spring bank holiday Monday each year. Contestants plunge heroically from the maypole down the slope in pursuit of a mock cheese, the winner taking home a real 7lb (3kg) Double Gloucester as the prize. In about 500BC Cooper's Hill was part of a large Iron Age encampment.

The route continues now through more woodland. With your back to the view as you stand beside the maypole, you will see two paths ahead. Take the one that angles half-right and follow it into the woods. On coming to a junction of tracks take the lower of two going off to the left. Brockworth and Buckholt Woods are linked by a short and narrow 'corridor' which is clearly waymarked. ▸

Almost as soon as you enter the second wood the path forks. Take the left branch and continue. At the next fork take the right-hand option ahead. The way broadens and more alternative paths and tracks are seen, but at

Designation as a national nature reserve acts as a protection for much of these woodlands, and in springtime they display a rich profusion of shade-loving plants amidst the birch, sycamore, beech and ash.

69

The top of the cheese-rolling slope on Cooper's Hill is a splendid viewpoint

Prinknash Abbey lies down the slope, ½ mile (800m) to the north, where refreshments can be had at the visitor centre.

each junction there are waymarks to direct you. On coming to a sign announcing Buckholt Wood Nature Reserve the path forks once more. Take the right-hand option which eases downhill to an unclassified road. Turn right and in a few paces you will reach a junction with the A46 (grid ref: 883131). This is sometimes referred to as Cranham Corner, sometimes as Prinknash Corner. ◄

Cross the A46 half-left ahead to find a continuing footpath with CW waymarks directing you once more into woodland. For about 100 metres you wander beside a drystone wall that forms a boundary to Prinknash Park, then leave it to bear left up a slope along a minor path. Within a few paces cross another unclassified road and walk straight on along the track which runs parallel with the A46 heading south-west.

This woodland (Pope's Wood) is part of Buckholt Wood Nature Reserve and it has a fine selection of deciduous trees and ground-covering plants. The track leads through it to a narrow metalled lane which in turn brings you out of the woods at last, and onto a golf course.

Waymarks initially lead to a clear track which maintains a fairly straight course between the fairways, keeping left of the undulations of **Painswick Beacon** (grid ref: 867121). It's worth making a slight diversion onto the summit of this hill, at 928 ft (283m), for extensive views across the Severn Vale.

PAINSWICK BEACON

Painswick Beacon has many other names: Painswick Hill (OS map), the Castles, Castle Godwyn and Kimsbury Hill. Overlooking Gloucester and the Severn Vale it was settled as a hill fort by late Iron Age tribes, used in 1052 as a temporary camp by Earl Godwyn (a Saxon leader in conflict with the Earl of Mercia), and again in 1643 by Royalist forces following the lifting of the Siege of Gloucester. The 250 acres (101 hectares) of common land are speckled with birches and trim with the manicured greens and fairways of Painswick Hill Golf Club.

Keeping to the waymarked route, views are given off to the left (south and east) across a green valley with yet more woods on the far side. On coming to a narrow lane cutting across the golf course, bear left and, a few paces later, go to the right on a broad track which you soon leave for a footpath half-left ahead, passing Catsbrain Quarry. The way leads along the edge of the hill slope, once again in woodland but with more lovely tree-framed views to enjoy.

When you emerge from the woods, cross an open stretch of golf-course fairway to the right-hand corner of a churchyard wall. Now continue with the wall to your left, passing the church which serves the hamlet of Paradise – so-called, it is said, because when he came here during the Civil War, Charles I thought the little hamlet to be just like the paradise of his dreams. Cross a further section of golf course towards the left-hand end of a woodland corner. Here a path accompanies a narrow lane most of the way to a junction with the B4073, where you turn left and stroll downhill into Painswick.

Follow Gloucester Road (it's named Gloucester

Street at the bottom end!) towards the centre of town. On coming to a crossroads turn right into New Street. But for a more interesting detour through the town, cross over New Street into Bisley Street, then bear right into Friday Street which leads to St Mary's Street, and on to the gracefully spired St Mary's Church. Rejoin the main route in New Street on the other side of the church by wandering through the churchyard and out at the lych gate (grid ref: 866097).

Painswick has a good choice of accommodation and refreshments. There's a small supermarket and a post office, and bus links with Cheltenham and Stroud.

PAINSWICK

Painswick is a delightful old market town and, like Chipping Campden at the start of the walk, a small one at that. But unlike the honey-gold of Campden, Painswick's stone is strangely white, or light grey, in colour. As a result the houses appear a little more formal than those of Campden, yet Painswick has much of merit and is worthy of more than a transitory glance. Dating from the 13th century, New Street is one of the town's oldest, but other streets –

The white stone of Painswick is one of the town's main features

Clipped yew hedges and table tombs in Painswick churchyard

notably those that lie north-east of the church – are also worth exploring. Friday Street indicates the siting of the Friday market, while Bisley Street, the original main street when Painswick was merely a village named Wicke, has a collection of splendid old buildings, among the oldest in the town. At the top of Hale Lane the old town stocks remain.

In common with several other Cotswold towns, Painswick owes its elegance to the cloth trade, at the height of which 25 mills were being powered by local streams. In the Civil War Royalists attacked the town, damaging St Mary's Church with fire and cannonballs, marks of which are evident to this day. The churchyard is noted for its clipped yew trees, its Renaissance-style table tombs and the lych gate, whose timbers, decorated with carvings of bells and music, came from the belfry roof after the spire collapsed in 1883. (At 174ft (53m) high, the elegant spire can be seen from a great distance, while the church it advertises is a true gem.) Each September a clipping ceremony takes place around the church – not the clipping of the churchyard yews, but a ceremony based on the Saxon word for embracing (*ycleping*), when the congregation joins hands to encircle the church while singing a special hymn. Tourist information: Painswick Library, Stroud Road, Painswick ☎01452 813552.

SECTION 7

Painswick to Middleyard
(King's Stanley)

Distance	9½ miles (15km)
Maps	Harvey's Cotswold Way 1:40,000
	OS Landranger 162 Gloucester & Forest of Dean Area 1:50,000
	OS Explorer 179 Gloucester, Cheltenham & Stroud 1:25,000
Accommodation	Edge, Haresfield (+ ¾ mile (1km)), Randwick (+ ½ mile (800m)), King's Stanley and Middleyard
Refreshments	Edge and Painswick

Open meadows, woodland shade, a sloping common scattered with birches, and some of the finest views of the whole Cotswold Way make this stage memorable for its variety.

Leaving Painswick the route heads westward over undulating farmland, across the Gloucester-to-Stroud road and up to Scottsquar Hill, with its quarry remains and a clear view back to Painswick. It then passes along the edge of an extensive stretch of woodland, broken here and there with occasional views north and west, before climbing onto the jutting prow of Haresfield Beacon where a vast panorama, lit by the meanderings of the River Severn, lies stretched before you. This green belvedere invites you to rest, to sit and enjoy its gift of space – a fine picnic spot. From Haresfield Beacon the way now breaks to the south, making a short diversion onto a neighbouring hill-top spur in order to benefit from more of the magnificent vista, before dropping among ancient woodlands again, well to the west of Stroud.

Stroud dominates a bowl of countryside above the River Frome, but the route keeps its distance and remains distinctly rural, passing through one or two outlying villages, crossing the Stroudwater Canal and, at King's Stanley, ending in a final meadowland stroll to Middleyard below wooded Pen Hill.

A longer, optional alternative route alongside the Stroudwater Canal and onto Selsley Common has been opened, and this is described on page 80. However, it avoids King's Stanley and Middleyard, where accommodation and refreshments are available.

From the lych gate on the New Street side of St Mary's Church in Painswick, cross to the narrow Edge Road and wander uphill along it, enjoying pleasant views off to the left as you gain height. After about 250 metres turn left into Hambutts Field (owned by the Open Spaces Society). Wander down its left-hand side, then go through a kissing gate and along an enclosed footpath at the back of houses, before emerging to an open sloping meadow. Walk down this to another kissing gate near the corner of a tennis court, then continue along the left-hand edge of a meadow for about 50 metres. Here you veer half-right to the bottom right-hand corner where you'll find another gate. The continuing path takes you over a stream and onto a track by the 17th-century grey stone Washbrook Farm, a former cloth mill that later changed to milling flour, but does neither now (grid ref: 857095).

The birch-clad slopes of Scottsquar Hill provide long vistas across a tranquil landscape

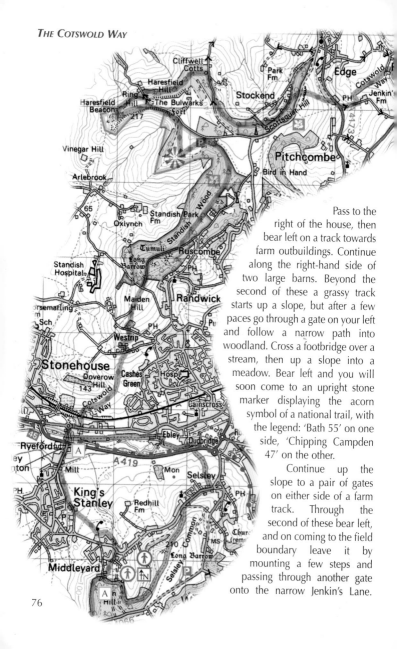

Pass to the right of the house, then bear left on a track towards farm outbuildings. Continue along the right-hand side of two large barns. Beyond the second of these a grassy track starts up a slope, but after a few paces go through a gate on your left and follow a narrow path into woodland. Cross a footbridge over a stream, then up a slope into a meadow. Bear left and you will soon come to an upright stone marker displaying the acorn symbol of a national trail, with the legend: 'Bath 55' on one side, 'Chipping Campden 47' on the other.

Continue up the slope to a pair of gates on either side of a farm track. Through the second of these bear left, and on coming to the field boundary leave it by mounting a few steps and passing through another gate onto the narrow Jenkin's Lane.

Walk up the lane to its junction with the A4173 Gloucester-to-Stroud road near the Edgemoor Inn (the village of Edge lies a short distance along this road to the right).

Turn right along the pavement for a few paces, then cross the road with great care to a gate opposite the pub. The waymarked path now takes you onto Edge Common, and over a crossing path ascends the slope among scatterings of silver birch (a bird-happy stretch). Coming onto Scottsquar Hill, you gain a charming view of Painswick gleaming white, backed, far off, by the folds of green and pleasant hills. ▸

Scottsquar Hill bears the scars of old quarries, and between the hilltop and a narrow lane to the west, the continuing path rises and falls among its rough undulations, finally leaving the common by way of steps leading up to a country lane. Cross this and go straight ahead where the way is signed to Haresfield Beacon. A narrow path descends through Stockend Wood (National Trust owned) and brings you to a farm track where you bear left. After passing two or three houses the track narrows, and then continues through more woods. (Being a bridleway, this track can be quite muddy at times.) Eventually you come to a narrow lane where you maintain direction, and almost immediately have more fine views to the right, across an indented coombe drained by Daniel's Brook, to the curving escarpment in the east. Scattered below, among the soft green meadows, typical Cotswold stone cottages and farms appear toy-like in the distance.

About 350 metres along the lane come to Cliffwell Cottages on the left, named after the well in its stone-built housing nearby. ▸

A path goes between the well and the cottage hedge and rises into Cliff Wood. The path curves round the scarp edge, and often grants lovely views between the trees. On a bend in the track you pass a stone commemorating the raising of the Siege of Gloucester on 5 September 1643 by the troops of Charles I. But why this

Cowslips and several varieties of orchids and herbs grow here, and the hillside attracts a population of various butterflies.

The inscription on the well-head is worth quoting: 'Whoer the Bucketful upwindeth, let him bless God, who water findest. Yet water here but small availeth. Go seek that well which never failest.'

Haresfield Beacon, a superb vantage point on the Cotswold Way

commemorative stone should be called Cromwell's Stone is unclear.

On coming to a small road opposite Ringhill Farm bear left for a few paces, then go to the right, through a metal field gate and along a track winding uphill beside a Dutch barn. At another field gate take the path along the right-hand side of a fence, and on to the trig point at the promontory end of Ring Hill, known here as **Haresfield Beacon** (grid ref: 820088). This exquisite spot rewards with a magnificent broad panorama overlooking the Vale of Gloucester, the River Severn, and the Forest of Dean rimming the horizon. The Severn glistens and gleams as it sweeps in huge oxbows out to the west.

HARESFIELD BEACON

Haresfield Beacon is a splendid promontory viewpoint at the tip of Ring Hill, on which there was once a hill fort of 10 acres (4 hectares). We know that the Romans were here, because excavations at the eastern end of the hill in 1837 unearthed traces of a Roman building and a pot containing nearly 3000 coins.

There are green vales and meadows below, woods and hedgerows darkening the landscape with strips and cloud-like shadows far off. There are distant towns and villages and isolated farms, but each in its place. It is all so orderly and set out in such artistic proportions – a lovely, gentle, very English landscape.

Facing the view, turn left at the trig point, walk along the scarp edge with the slope falling to your right, and note across the indented vale another projecting spur which you will visit next. Pass through a gate onto a fence-guided path that takes you among trees and then out to the edge of a road by a parking area. Without going onto the road, cut away to the right on a waymarked descent of a series of wood-braced steps and a path that winds left along the lower terrace of hillside. The way soon begins to reclaim lost height and emerges to a large open meadowland. Bear half-right across this to reach a topograph with more superb views to enjoy, complementing those of Haresfield Beacon a short distance away to the north-west.

Return from the topograph by cutting back hard left on a faint path across the grassland to reach the National Trust's Cripplegate car park, which you leave by a gap in the wall on the right. Here you enter ancient Standish Wood, mentioned in a document of 1297. Almost at once the track forks three ways. Take the left-hand trail and follow this deeply into the woods. There are many alternative side tracks and junctions, but on coming to each one, CW marker posts direct you along the correct path. Eventually the Cotswold Way joins a bridleway and slopes downhill to emerge from the woods. As you leave the trees, Stroud is seen sprawling in its valley below.

Coming to the head of a small road leading to Randwick, cross directly ahead, go through a gate into a meadow, and follow a stone wall beyond which there are more fine views. Pass through a second gate and continue into another meadow where you bear half-left to locate a stone stile at the top end of a wall, and take the footpath through Three Bears Wood.

At the end of this small woodland veer left on a narrow lane by some houses. Shortly after, turn right through a gap into a meadowland where the continuing path goes straight ahead. Waymarks guide you down to more houses on yet another narrow road where you turn right. Walk uphill for about 200 metres, then bear left over a stile and cut through a field to a squeeze stile found beneath an oak tree. Continue in the same direction, pass beneath some power cables and, in a dip, cross a stile by a field gate, then follow the left-hand boundary hedge of the field beyond.

ALTERNATIVE ROUTE

Immediately after crossing the Stroudwater Canal turn left onto the canal-side footpath. From here to an abandoned lock, the canal is green with algae, a rather sad and neglected sight. But it is even worse beyond the old lock, for the path takes you through a stretch of scrubland below gardens, with a few damp areas showing where the canal once led. Across a narrow service road come to a short section of open water, but you soon leave it for a footpath heading to the right. This takes you across a bridge spanning the little River Frome and into a field.

Bear left through linking fields heading upstream until you're almost opposite Ebley Mill. Here you climb a flight of wooden steps on the right to a tarmac path above the A419. Turn left for a short distance, then cross the road at pedestrian-controlled traffic lights, angle up a slope and enter a meadow via a kissing gate. Marker posts direct the way across two sections of meadow before bringing you to a minor road at Selsley.

Turn right alongside the road towards Selsley church, and on coming to the junction with The Grove cross to a gate, through which you then climb the slope leading onto the lovely open flank of Selsley Common. The path takes you along the west flank just below the crest of the hill (with huge views to enjoy), until you come to the edge of Pen Wood. The way now goes down a slope to a path junction, then keeps ahead through the woods.

After crossing a drive, wind along the slopes of Pen Hill to a signed junction at grid ref: 818027. The right-hand option offers a descent to Middleyard and King's Stanley for accommodation and refreshments, but the continuing route veers left and is signed to Coaley Peak (2 miles). For the remainder of the walk to Dursley please turn to page 83.

After two sides of the field you come to another squeeze stile. Maintain direction through two more fields, then find a footbridge leading from the middle of the left-hand boundary hedge of the third field, over the Stroud-to-Gloucester railway line, and down the edge of a sports field. On coming to the B4008 opposite a garden centre, turn right and walk along the pavement to a road junction with a dimple roundabout. Cross with care and wander down Ryeford Road North in the direction of Ryeford. This takes you over the Stroudwater Canal and, soon after, brings you to the A419. ▶

Cross at the pedestrian traffic lights, then walk ahead along Ryeford Road South. This takes you past the now-obsolete **Stanley Mill** on the edge of King's Stanley village (grid ref: 813043).

The **Stroudwater Canal** was opened in 1779 to service the industrialised Stroud Valley. It was only 8 miles (12½km) long, but it linked Stroud town with the navigable River Severn at Upper Framilode by way of a dozen locks.

STANLEY MILL

Constructed in 1811, Stanley Mill is a five-storey brick-and-stone building whose great looms were originally powered by no less than five water-wheels. These gave way to steam power in 1827. Within its first 20 years the mill employed almost 1000 workers.

On the left of the road now, waymarks take you through a gate and along the left-hand edge of a long field. At the end go through another gate and maintain direction through a second field. Halfway through this second field the path forks. Take the right branch, and on the far side go through yet another gate. The way now eases to the right among bushes, and brings you close to a footbridge over a stream. Do not cross, but veer left, and via yet another gate, walk alongside a garden boundary. At the far end come to a crossing path and turn left. ▶

Cross a farm drive, and through another gate turn half-right across a field, then round the edge of two more fields before leaving through a squeeze stile to emerge beside King's Stanley Baptist Church in Middleyard (grid ref: 820032).

Note If you need accommodation or refreshments in King's Stanley, turn right here and you will soon arrive in the village via a playing field.

SECTION 8

Middleyard (King's Stanley) to Dursley

Distance	6½ miles (10½km)
Maps	Harvey's Cotswold Way 1:40,000
	OS Landranger 162 Gloucester & Forest of Dean Area 1:50,000
	OS Explorer 168 Stroud, Tetbury & Malmesbury, and 167 Thornbury, Dursley & Yate 1:25,000
Accommodation	Uley and Dursley
Refreshments	None until Dursley

This short stage is strenuous in places, with a fair amount of height to be gained and lost. There are interesting archaeological sites to be seen, more extensive views, woodland walks and that finest of all outliers, Cam Long Down, to be crossed.

Climbing out of Middleyard, the way soon plunges into beech woods for a long traverse of hillside, but when it finally emerges onto Frocester Hill near the Nympsfield Long Barrow, a splendid open panorama comes as a welcome gift. Cam Long Down and Cam Peak (or Peaked Down according to the Ordnance Survey) are seen clearly from here: two isolated hills (outliers) that have become separated from the main escarpment, they appear like landlocked islands rising from the Vale of Berkeley to the south-west. The route passes near Hetty Pegler's Tump, another Neolithic long barrow, and Uleybury promontory fort which was created during the Iron Age. Short diversions are recommended to look at both these ancient sites. The way-marked route slopes down the steep scarp face, then cuts westward to make the ascent of Cam Long Down, before descending by a cross-country route into Dursley, a busy little town wedged between the wolds.

Where the path brings the Cotswold Way into Middleyard beside King's Stanley Baptist Church, turn left and walk along the road for about 50 metres, then cross

to the right into a very narrow drive beside Rosebank Cottage. When it curves a little to the left, branch right on a continuing drive, passing a house and coming to an enclosed footpath rising steadily among trees. The path brings you to a sloping meadow which you cross diagonally to its top right-hand corner. Turn left on a metalled lane, and a few paces later take an enclosed path half-left ahead to pass Brushwood Cottage.

The tree-crowned outlier of Downham Hill is seen from the slopes of Cam Long Down

When you come to the edge of woods hugging Pen Hill, bear right and follow a fence. As the slope eases, contour along the hillside on a lovely woodland path among tall, straight, green-trunked beeches that look wonderful in autumn. After some time the path is joined by another coming from the left. Continue ahead, but shortly after meeting a second junction the way eases downhill, narrows, and then emerges from the woods onto a grassy hillside. Views ahead include the River Severn.

Maintain direction across the slope, pass above Woodside Farm then, after hugging the woodland edge for a while, enter Stanley Wood by way of a kissing gate. Keep straight ahead, rising gently, then over a crossing track to continue gaining height. After a while the

83

NYMPSFIELD LONG BARROW

Nympsfield Long Barrow is similar in concept to many Neolithic barrows of the Severn-Cotswold Group. Constructed around 2800BC it was used for burials and, probably, as a place of ritual. The site was first excavated in the 19th century, when the remains of 13 people, together with a flint arrowhead and some pottery, were discovered in the pair of side chambers that lead from the main passageway. The barrow has obviously deteriorated over the years, and the drystone walling is merely a reconstruction.

woodland path makes a more gentle contour round the hillside, going among trees with just sufficient space between them to allow glimpsed views out to the right. There are several crossing tracks and path junctions, but CW waymarks keep you on the correct line. The upper hillside eases and you discover that the path is running parallel with a road. Waymarks direct you along the fenced edge of a small wooded quarry on the right, soon after which you leave the woods and come out on an open grassy space at Coaley Peak Picnic Site.

Cross the open meadow to pass alongside the **Nympsfield Long Barrow** (grid ref: 794015),

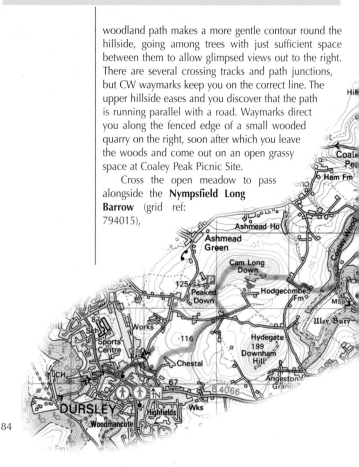

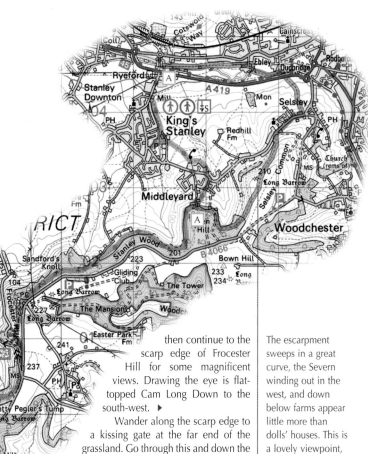

then continue to the scarp edge of Frocester Hill for some magnificent views. Drawing the eye is flat-topped Cam Long Down to the south-west. ▶

Wander along the scarp edge to a kissing gate at the far end of the grassland. Go through this and down the slope a little, keeping to the lower path when it forks. Another kissing gate takes the way among trees and scrub. Pass an exposed section of limestone cliff, beyond which the path then works its way up a series of stone steps and onto a road. Bear left. In a few paces come to the B4066 where you head to the right – **Hetty Pegler's Tump** is not far away. A short distance along the road a Cotswold Way signpost directs a bridlepath down into woodlands. ▶

The escarpment sweeps in a great curve, the Severn winding out in the west, and down below farms appear little more than dolls' houses. This is a lovely viewpoint, worth giving time to absorb.

Note To visit Hetty Pegler's Tump continue along the roadside for a further ½ mile (800m).

HETTY PEGLER'S TUMP

Hetty Pegler's Tump is found just off the route of the Cotswold Way to the south of Nympsfield Long Barrow. This Neolithic burial mound is in very good condition. Measuring 140ft long by 90ft wide (42m x 27m), the covering mound is about 10ft (3m) high. From a long internal passageway there are two pairs of side chambers and a single chamber at the western end. The two northern chambers have been sealed off. Nineteenth-century excavations unearthed pieces of Roman pottery and an Edward IV silver groat. The mound (or tump) gained its curious name because it stands on land that was owned in the 17th century by Henry and Hester (or Hetty) Pegler.

The Cotswold Way descends the steep scarp face along a stony bridleway. When it forks take the upper option, now on a footpath. After going through a gate the way rises then contours along the wooded hillside. Another gate is met at a junction of paths. Here you veer left, rise a little then contour once more below an exposed quarried cliff before coming to a broad crossing track near road-level at Crawley Barns not far from **Uleybury Hill Fort**. (To visit the fort simply go up a little further to the left. The ramparts of this ancient site make for an interesting circuit.)

To continue the route, cross the broad track and descend the bridleway opposite. It soon becomes embedded in a gully-like sunken track, then emerges at the foot of the slope between Springfield and Hodgecombe Farms (accommodation). This is a beautiful, peaceful location with splendid views.

ULEYBURY HILL FORT

The hill fort occupies more than 30 acres (12 hectares) of land on the very edge of the escarpment south-east of Cam Long Down. Dating from the Iron Age it is certainly an impressive and well-chosen site as it has a 300ft (91m) drop down the scarp face to help protect it. A ditch and rampart complete the defences. Uleybury has never been excavated, although second- and fourth-century Roman coins have been found here.

Go ahead on the track towards Cam Long Down. The track veers left to a narrow country lane where you bear right for about 100 metres or so until coming to some barns. Go through a gate and continue ahead following the right-hand fence. A stile takes you out of the field and onto the lower meadow slopes of **Cam Long Down**. There are very fine views left to the attractive tree-crowned outlier of Downham Hill. Climb directly ahead up the steep slope to find a stile and steps under an oak tree. The way now winds up through a little wooded area on numerous steps, and emerges onto the summit.

CAM LONG DOWN

The impressive outlier of Cam Long Down came into being, according to legend, when the Devil decided to dam the River Severn and drown the people of Gloucestershire in revenge for their having built too many churches. Above Dursley he filled his wheelbarrow with a great chunk of the Cotswolds, but while resting from his labours along came a cobbler with a string of shoes to be mended draped around his neck. When the Devil asked for directions to the river, the suspicious cobbler explained that it was so far that he had already worn out several pairs of shoes on the way from it. The Devil lost heart and emptied his wheelbarrow-load of stone which became, of course, Cam Long Down. (Similar folk legends occur all over the country.) Strip lynchets (terraces or ridges) may be seen on the south-facing slopes, while the summit plateau is rumpled with strange undulations that indicate the possible existence of some form of ancient settlement.

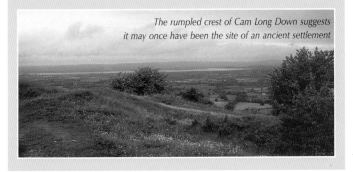

The rumpled crest of Cam Long Down suggests it may once have been the site of an ancient settlement

A wonderful panorama is to be seen from here: the windings of the Severn to the west, now a wide river of substance with the Forest of Dean as backing, the curving Cotswold escarpment, the clustered streets of Dursley below to the south-west, and Downham Hill to the south. There are more tiny villages to the north, green meadows set between hedgerow envelopes, and a wonderful sense of space.

Cross the ridge to its western end, then begin the descent to Dursley. The path soon forks, and you take the left branch which leads to a multi-junction of paths on the saddle connecting Cam Long Down with Cam Peak (Peaked Down). Go half-left ahead on a minor path to skirt the lower, southern slope of **Cam Peak**, and very soon you'll come alongside a fence. About 50 metres later cross a stile on the left, then walk down the left-hand edge of a sloping meadow, at the bottom of which you come to a lane by farm buildings.

CAM PEAK

Cam Peak (Peaked Down on the OS maps) is a secondary hill of 604ft (184m) standing just to the south-west of Cam Long Down to which it is connected. The former route of the Cotswold Way crossed its summit, and gives similar magnificent views to those of its neighbour. It is still worth making a diversion to the top – an obvious path climbs to it from the saddle between the two peaks.

Cross the lane half-right ahead onto a streamside path which takes you behind some houses and into a meadow. Keep ahead along the left-hand edge, enter a second meadow and maintain direction, soon losing the stream which curves leftward. The path now rises slightly through the meadow to its opposite boundary fence where you turn left. After about 100 metres go through a gate on the right and walk along the top boundary of another meadow. Following a fence, keep on to the far corner where you enter a very small meadow. Veer slightly left to a gateway, then continue through parkland

DURSLEY

Once one of the principal wool and cloth towns of the Cotswolds, with the decline in woollen manufacture Dursley made a successful transition to modern engineering. Transition seems to be in the blood of the town, for Roger Berkeley, cousin to Edward the Confessor, held the manor of Dursley and had built himself a castle (long since disappeared) by the time the Normans landed, but rather than be replaced by a favourite of the invaders, he managed to retain his position. Eventually manorial ties were severed and the new masters were those whose power came from wool. Now, as elsewhere along the Cotswolds, the dependence on sheep is but a memory. However, the town survives in its own right, although the price for survival has been the substitution of a number of old buildings by others of less architectural merit. Nonetheless, the Market House (built 1738) remains a model of a past era. It has a bell turret, and a niche with a statue of Queen Anne which faces the church.

The old Market House in Dursley, built in 1738

Autumn colours add the Midas touch to the Cotswold Way

(the way is not very clear) towards its far bottom corner where a kissing gate gives onto a drive. Turn right and follow this down to Long Street in **Dursley**, which you gain beside a building known as the Priory. Walk up Long Street to reach the covered Market House in the town centre (grid ref: 757982). Dursley has a range of accommodation, refreshments, shops, a post office, and so on.

SECTION 9

Dursley to Wotton-under-Edge

Distance	7 miles (11km)
Maps	Harvey's Cotswold Way 1:40,000
	OS Landranger 162 Gloucester & Forest of
	Dean Area 1:50,000
	OS Explorer 167 Thornbury, Dursley & Yate 1:25,000
Accommodation	North Nibley and Wotton-under-Edge
Refreshments	North Nibley and Wotton-under-Edge

The way continues to explore the western edge of the escarpment, with wide vistas that include the River Severn and Forest of Dean. There's a section of low-lying farmland to cross, but in itself this is as interesting as the scarp edge. By contrast with the previous walk, on this stage there is only one prehistoric site – the hill fort of Brackenbury Ditches. This is to the south of the lofty Tyndale Monument, built to commemorate the life of William Tyndale, who translated the Bible into English.

From Dursley a steep climb through woodland leads onto Stinchcombe Hill, where a circuit of the plateau is made which reveals one of the finest of all Cotswold panoramas. Then follows a descent over an agricultural landscape to the little village of North Nibley. Another climb takes you back to the escarpment by the Tyndale Monument on Nibley Knoll, continues through Westridge Wood, and then past Brackenbury Ditches. Wotton Hill comes next, with its circular enclosure of the Jubilee Plantation, from which you gain a splendid overview of Wotton-under-Edge. A steep path then descends into this old wool town to make a fitting conclusion to the day.

To leave Dursley walk through the pedestrian shopping precinct behind the old Market House, and at the far end go left into May Lane. Leave this when Hill Road branches from it by the Old Spot pub. Wander up Hill Road, but when it swings left, go ahead on a track on the edge of woodland. In a few paces branch half-left ahead

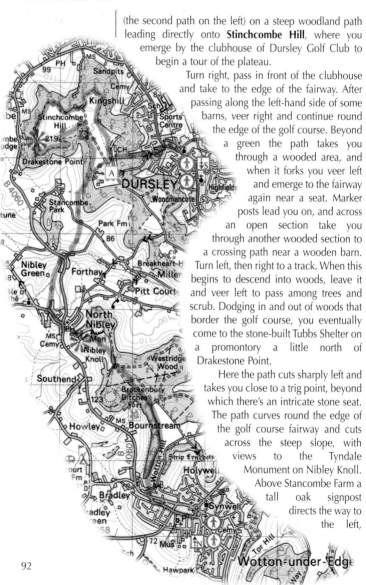

(the second path on the left) on a steep woodland path leading directly onto **Stinchcombe Hill**, where you emerge by the clubhouse of Dursley Golf Club to begin a tour of the plateau.

Turn right, pass in front of the clubhouse and take to the edge of the fairway. After passing along the left-hand side of some barns, veer right and continue round the edge of the golf course. Beyond a green the path takes you through a wooded area, and when it forks you veer left and emerge to the fairway again near a seat. Marker posts lead you on, and across an open section take you through another wooded section to a crossing path near a wooden barn. Turn left, then right to a track. When this begins to descend into woods, leave it and veer left to pass among trees and scrub. Dodging in and out of woods that border the golf course, you eventually come to the stone-built Tubbs Shelter on a promontory a little north of Drakestone Point.

Here the path cuts sharply left and takes you close to a trig point, beyond which there's an intricate stone seat. The path curves round the edge of the golf course fairway and cuts across the steep slope, with views to the Tyndale Monument on Nibley Knoll. Above Stancombe Farm a tall oak signpost directs the way to the left,

STINCHCOMBE HILL

Given to the public by Sir Stanley Tubbs in 1930, Stinchcombe Hill is a magnificent vantage point, with numerous outlooks from the scarp edge, and with a topograph near Drakestone Point highlighting some of the main features in the panorama. These include Berkeley Castle, the Malvern Hills, the Brecon Beacons, and even Exmoor, which it is claimed can be seen from here.

SHORTCUT

For the shortcut, bear left at the clubhouse, turn right onto a narrow road, then almost immediately leave the tarmac to take a line across the left-hand edge of a fairway. Marker posts guide this shortcut, and direct you to the point at which the Cotswold Way proper enters woodland for a steep descent that eventually leads to North Nibley.

passing through another brief section of woodland before coming onto the fairway once more. Yet more marker posts lead the way to a fine signpost on the edge of woods, where the alternative shortcut route from the clubhouse joins the main Cotswold Way. Turn right here and descend the steep wooded slope.

Near the foot of the slope leave the bridleway for a path on the left which crosses a gully by some gas pipes. The way now cuts across sloping fields to a stile leading onto the narrow Park Lane (grid ref: 743972). Turn left, and a few paces later go through a kissing gate on the right into a large field. A signpost here directs the route to North Nibley. Walk through the middle of the field and out again by way of a stile on the far side, then straight ahead to the edge of a steep slope. The continuing path goes half-right, crosses another stile and comes out onto a lane by some cottages. Bear right along the lane as far as a road junction.

Cross straight ahead onto a bridleway among trees. Along this trackway you will pass an old doorway, dated 1607, in the right-hand wall, of which little appears to be

93

Nibley Knoll, with the prominent Tyndale Monument, is a focus of attention from Stinchcombe Hill

known. The way narrows to become almost a tunnel, then emerges to a lane in front of houses. Continue straight ahead, then bear left into The Street in **North Nibley**, which has bed-and-breakfast accommodation, refreshments at the Black Horse Inn, and a shop (grid ref: 740958).

NORTH NIBLEY

North Nibley is 'The clearing near the peak'. Among its oldest dwellings is Nibley House, which was partially rebuilt in 1763 from an earlier house. Set back a little from the main village, the Church of St Martin is a fine building that dates from the 15th century. Nearby is Nibley Green, where the last battle to be fought in England between private armies took place in 1470 between the Berkeleys and the Lisles. About 2000 men took part and Lord Lisle, who had challenged Lord Berkeley to do battle over the ownership of Berkeley Castle, was shot first in the face then stabbed to death. His retainer army fled and was scattered over the surrounding countryside, while his house was sacked by Berkeley's men. Around 150 men died in this senseless conflict.

The Street leads to the B4060 opposite the Black Horse Inn. Turn right and walk alongside the road as far as a telephone box, then cross to the left where the Cotswold Way continues as a classic sunken track going up to Nibley Knoll and the Tyndale Monument. (The monument is kept locked, but if you wish to climb it to the top, note the location of the key, which is given on a noticeboard at the foot of the track.) A few paces along the track, leave it for a long flight of steps that climbs the wooded slope and emerges on a hilltop meadow by the tall grey tower of the **Tyndale Monument**, solemn-looking with iron railings round the base and a cross on top. A nearby topograph highlights major items in the huge view, including the Severn Bridge, 12 miles (19km) away, and Haresfield Beacon, the latter having been visited on Section 7, now 10 miles (16km) distant as the crow flies, but no less than 18 miles (29km) along the Cotswold Way.

TYNDALE MONUMENT

The Tyndale Monument on Nibley Knoll is a prominent and impressive landmark that can be seen from a huge distance. Standing 111 ft (34m) high, it was designed by S. S. Teulon, and erected in 1866 in memory of William Tyndale who translated the Bible into English. While a plaque here suggests he was born at North Nibley, there is no firm evidence to substantiate this claim. Apparently a Tyndale did live nearby at about the right time, but he was not even related to the William Tyndale who was born in 1484 and martyred in Flanders on 6 October 1536.

From the monument bear left along the scarp edge (more fine views) to find the entrance to Westridge Wood. Inside the wood there are numerous crossing tracks and side paths, but at each junction CW waymarks guide you. On the route through you pass the site of **Brackenbury Ditches** just to the right.

The path leaves the wood but then continues alongside it, following the right-hand boundary of a large field. At the far corner a kissing gate takes the path into a small

BRACKENBURY DITCHES

Brackenbury Ditches is the name given to another Iron Age hill fort, rather overgrown with trees, but not entirely hidden. The outer defensive ditch has been cleared, but presumably because of the dense woodland cover within, the site has never been excavated. Nearby, at a junction of paths in Westridge Wood, the outlawed practice of cock-fighting used to take place.

promontory meadow (Wotton Hill) marked by a clump of commemorative trees set within a circular wall. This is known as the **Jubilee Plantation**, and from it there are very fine views overlooking Wotton-under-Edge.

JUBILEE PLANTATION

The Jubilee Plantation on Wotton Hill was planted initially to celebrate the victory against Napoleon at Waterloo in 1815, but in order to mark the end of the Crimean War the trees were felled for a bonfire. The circular wall was erected and more trees planted in 1887 to celebrate Queen Victoria's golden jubilee. Yet more planting took place in 1952.

The steep descending path drops down the forward left-hand slope of this promontory meadow. A waymark post directs from below, and on the way to it care should be exercised, especially if the grass is damp. A kissing gate and a set of steps lead onto a lane. Go straight across and down the continuing footpath which brings you to a road leading left into **Wotton-under-Edge**, where there is a choice of accommodation, refreshments, shops, a post office, and so on.

At the first junction bear right. The road curves round to become the High Street, and this in turn comes to Long Street. From here bear left into Church Street, then right at the bottom to take a raised footpath leading to an alleyway called the Cloud, which leads to a crossing alleyway (Shinbone Alley). Turn left and wander up to the churchyard of the handsome Parish Church of St Mary the Virgin (grid ref: 760935).

WOTTON-UNDER-EDGE

First mentioned in a royal charter dated AD940 – its Saxon name means 'the farm in the wood'. The original village was almost completely destroyed by fire during the reign of King John as a reprisal for Lord Berkeley's part in the lead up to Magna Carta. The rebuilt town achieved the status of a borough in 1253, and grew to become an important wool town with several productive mills situated along the stream that runs through it. The Parish Church of St Mary the Virgin is worth visiting. Dating from 1283 it is said to replace one that was destroyed during the earlier burning of the town. Katherine, Lady Berkeley, has a fine brass. It was she who gave Wotton the distinction of having the first school founded by a woman (in 1384). Isaac Pitman, who developed his shorthand system here, was the first master at another Wotton school, the British School on the corner of Bear Lane. The oldest house in the town is said to be the former Ram Inn (built 1350, to the south of the church), while the 17th-century gabled almshouses in Church Street have within their courtyard a lovely chapel containing some splendid stained glass. All in all the town is a pleasing mixture of past and present, tucked against the wooded wolds. Tourist information: The Heritage Centre, The Chipping, Wotton-under-Edge ☎01453 521541.

Church Street, Wotton-under-Edge

97

SECTION 10

Wotton-Under-Edge to Hawkesbury Upton

Distance	8 miles (12½km)
Maps	Harvey's Cotswold Way 1:40,000
	OS Landranger 172 Bristol, Bath & Surrounding Area 1:50,000
	OS Explorer 167 Thornbury, Dursley & Yate 1:25,000
Accommodation	Alderley, Kilcott and Hawkesbury Upton
Refreshments	None until Hawkesbury Upton

The way approaches Alderley through a colourful tunnel of trees

On this stage of the walk one is reminded yet again of the district's past dependence on the wool and cloth industries, for in places the route leads through valleys and alongside streams whose power was formerly harnessed by cloth mills. Some of these mills are still to be seen today. Others which once lined the valleys disappeared with the coming of the Industrial Revolution. Though many of the mills may have gone, the valleys and their streams remain to give the walker a day of gentle pleasures.

But in spite of these valley sections the path does not completely desert the high wolds, for it is not long after leaving Wotton that the escarpment is gained once more. Yet again there are woodlands for company, and deep, sunken tracks to follow. More charming, typical Cotswold cottages adorn the lower slopes, and there's plenty of variety to maintain interest all the way. As the Cotswold crow flies, Hawkesbury Upton is barely 4 miles (6km) from Wotton, but the route doubles that distance without difficulty on its zigzag course along the scarp edge and in and out of 'back country' valleys.

From Wotton-under-Edge the route leads initially north-eastwards beside a lovely stream towards Coombe, then south and east steeply up Blackquarries Hill with views growing in extent once more. Round Wortley Hill and Tor Hill among woods, the way then descends a deep track to the edge of Wortley village. A cross-country section of agricultural land journeys to tiny Alderley, before following the millstream of Kilcott Brook through a lovely peaceful vale, then up to the Somerset Monument on the outskirts of Hawkesbury Upton. It is during this stage of the walk that the very nature of the Cotswold Way begins to change.

On leaving the churchyard of St Mary the Virgin, turn right and walk along the pavement a short distance before turning right into Valley Road. This curves to the left and brings you to a one-time millstream – a clear, friendly companion to follow for a while on a tarmac footpath. Cross a narrow lane at Holywell, and continue in the same direction to Coombe. On reaching a second narrow lane turn right, but coming to a house named The Hive leave the roadway and turn left on a bridleway rising steeply among trees, where the slopes are carpeted with ramsons in springtime. Still climbing, come to a lane where you turn left onto Blackquarries Hill.

Out of the trees the lane runs along the hilltop between fields. Follow this for a little over ½ mile (800m), but shortly after coming to a woodland on the left a track cuts sharply back to the right with a signpost indicating the way to Tor Hill and Alderley. Along this track the views take in the Tyndale Monument across Wotton's valley, and far beyond that to a succession of curving spurs and indents along the scarp slope.

When the track turns into a field on the left, continue straight ahead through a field gate to follow a crumbling wall. The wall curves left and ends, then a waymark directs you on a faint path across a sloping terrace of pasture, with the scarp edge plunging steeply away to the right. This is one of the last edges of the walk.

On the far side of the terrace go through a strip of woodland, by way of steps, to a track where you bear right. Losing height enter a plantation. Several alternative tracks break away, but waymarks keep you on course. When the main track skirts left, continue straight ahead on a narrow path which becomes a dark, deeply sunken track. Between steep banks draped with ivy and hart's tongue fern, with trees high overhead to complete the

WORTLEY AND ALDERLEY

Wortley and Alderley are small neighbouring villages astride a minor road that leads from Wotton to Hawkesbury Upton, but they can also be reached via devious footpath routes. Wortley was involved in the district's cloth trade by virtue of several mills powered by local streams. It is also famed as the birthplace of Stephen Hopkins, who made his fortune in that cloth trade and then sailed to America with the Pilgrim Fathers in 1620. He became an important official and died there in 1644.

Alderley is 'the clearing in the alders', a charming hamlet set on a spur of land between the Ozleworth and Kilcott valleys. Here lived a Lord Chief Justice, Matthew Hale (1609–76); a botanical artist, Marianne North (died 1890); and another eminent botanist, Brian Houghton Hodgson, who lived for a while at The Grange. But, long before all these, one Alderley inhabitant in the 13th century claimed to be the resurrected Christ, whereupon magistrates sent him to Oxford to be executed. Some say he died by crucifixion.

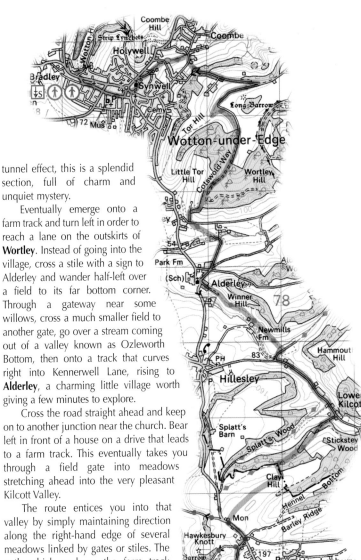

tunnel effect, this is a splendid section, full of charm and unquiet mystery.

Eventually emerge onto a farm track and turn left in order to reach a lane on the outskirts of **Wortley**. Instead of going into the village, cross a stile with a sign to Alderley and wander half-left over a field to its far bottom corner. Through a gateway near some willows, cross a much smaller field to another gate, go over a stream coming out of a valley known as Ozleworth Bottom, then onto a track that curves right into Kennerwell Lane, rising to **Alderley**, a charming little village worth giving a few minutes to explore.

Cross the road straight ahead and keep on to another junction near the church. Bear left in front of a house on a drive that leads to a farm track. This eventually takes you through a field gate into meadows stretching ahead into the very pleasant Kilcott Valley.

The route entices you into that valley by simply maintaining direction along the right-hand edge of several meadows linked by gates or stiles. The path which replaces the farm track eventually goes along a narrow, tree-enclosed section and on to a crossing

Kilcott Mill, one of several that used to power the local cloth trade

farm track, or green lane, where you turn right. Cross the Kilcott Brook and come to a country road where you bear left (grid ref: 779898).

With the Kilcott Brook for company, before long you pass Kilcott Mill with its pond and old stone buildings on your left. About ¾ mile (1km) after joining the road you come to the few cottages that comprise the hamlet of Lower Kilcott. Here a bridleway breaks away to the right along a sunken track. This is not only the route of the Cotswold Way, but is also shared by the **Monarch's Way**.

The track rises gently and forks. Branch left, still rising among trees, with the bank smothered in wild garlic. At the head of the slope go through a gateway and swing to the right, now walking along the top edge of a field. At the far end enter Claypit Wood on another track. At the western end of the wood come to a crossing track and bear left. Go up the slope alongside two narrow linking fields, at the top of which you turn right on another crossing track that takes you across Clay Hill (with big

MONARCH'S WAY

An epic, long-distance route of 609 miles (980km). Beginning in Worcester, it follows a meandering course to Shoreham, in Sussex, and is based on the journey taken by Charles II after his defeat at the Battle of Worcester in 1651. A three-volume route guide by Trevor Antill is published by Meridian Books.

views in all directions) and brings you directly to the imposing **Somerset Monument** northwest of Hawkesbury Upton. Turn left alongside a road. The Cotswold Way breaks to the right by a pond shortly after passing the village sign (grid ref: 774874). However, walkers in need of accommodation, refreshments, shop or post office should continue for about 400 metres beyond the pond to reach the heart of **Hawkesbury Upton**.

SOMERSET MONUMENT

The Somerset Monument dates from 1846 and was erected in memory of General Lord Somerset, a son of the fifth Duke of Beaufort, whose family seat was at nearby Badminton, of horse trials fame. General Somerset served under Wellington at the Battle of Waterloo, but whether this was commendable enough to warrant such a lofty memorial is questionable. It stands more than 120ft (36m) high and for a small fee you can climb the 144 steps to the viewing platform. It is also known as the Hawkesbury Monument.

*May blossom adds colour
and fragrance to a springtime
journey along the Cotswold Way*

HAWKESBURY UPTON

Hawkesbury Upton developed around a farm mentioned in a document of 972AD, but has grown very little since then during its thousand-year history. In fact its expansion has been surprisingly limited, considering its prominent position on the wolds just west of the Bath road, and most of the village buildings are less than a hundred years old.

SECTION 11

Hawkesbury Upton to Tormarton

Distance	8 miles (12½km)
Maps	Harvey's Cotswold Way 1:40,000
	OS Landranger 172 Bristol, Bath & Surrounding Area 1:50,000
	OS Explorer 167 Thornbury, Dursley & Yate, and 155 Bristol & Bath 1:25,000
Accommodation	Horton (+ ½ mile (800m)), Old Sodbury and Tormarton
Refreshments	Old Sodbury and Tormarton

Although there are a few small villages along this section of the route, it is very much a peaceful, seemingly remote stretch of countryside to wander through, and while it has none of the previous scarp-edge vastness of view, there are nevertheless vistas of great beauty to enjoy. The descent to Horton Court is a highlight, another is the visit to Sodbury Hill Fort, yet another the crossing of Dodington Park.

Within a few yards of rejoining the route by the pond in Hawkesbury Upton, the way travels along an old green lane called Bath Lane. I took this to be an apt name when tackling the route one autumn, for it was badly waterlogged from days of heavy rain and I waded through with no opportunity to dodge it, the water coming well above the top of my walking boots! (The name of the lane, of course, actually refers to the town of Bath at the end of an old trading route, of which this was but a section, and my subsequent walks along the track have been commendably dry.) The approach to Horton Court, coming off the hills near the end of Bath Lane, presents a broad panorama over low-lying land to the west, while from Horton to Little Sodbury you walk through what seems a 'lost' farmland dotted with sheep. Lanes and more field paths take the way from Little Sodbury to Old Sodbury, then on to graceful, pheasant-scurrying Dodington Park. Tormarton at the end of this stage shyly hides itself away from the busy A46 to the west, and the deep cut of the M4 to the south. Here, it seems, the Cotswolds have been lost and all but forgotten. Until the next stage, that is.

The village pond in Hawkesbury Upton is set in a triangle of roads. As you approach it from the Somerset Monument, turn right, then shortly after go left on a bridleway track signed to Horton. This is Bath Lane, which you follow to its end. Do not go onto the road (Highfield Lane) which crosses it, but bear right on a footpath that runs along the headland of two fields. On entering a third field, with a derelict stone-built barn seen ahead, bear half-right, pass a group of trees and bushes near the barn, go through a gap in the hedgerow and ahead along the right-hand edge of a large field. After about 100 metres veer right above a hollow where the way is guided by marker posts to the lower edge of a field. Enter woods through a gate and weave along the slope among fine trees (mostly beech), with masses of wild garlic adding pungency and thousands of beautiful white stars in spring-time. At a junction of paths bear slightly right, ignoring the broad descending path, and cut across the slope, soon leaving the woods by a kissing gate. Wander across a sloping field, with **Horton Court** seen below to the right and lovely views stretching ahead.

Map continues p.108

Go through another kissing gate on the far side of the field, up a zigzag path among bluebells through a belt of trees, then into a hilltop meadow. Walk ahead along the right-hand edge of the meadow with yet more beautiful views to enjoy to the west. Come to the earthworks of Horton Hill Fort and cut diagonally through it to the far left corner. Out by way of a gate, turn right and walk down the slope to pass a charming little stone tower, a folly built as a millennium project to encourage nesting barn owls and swallows. Along the bottom edge of the sloping meadow

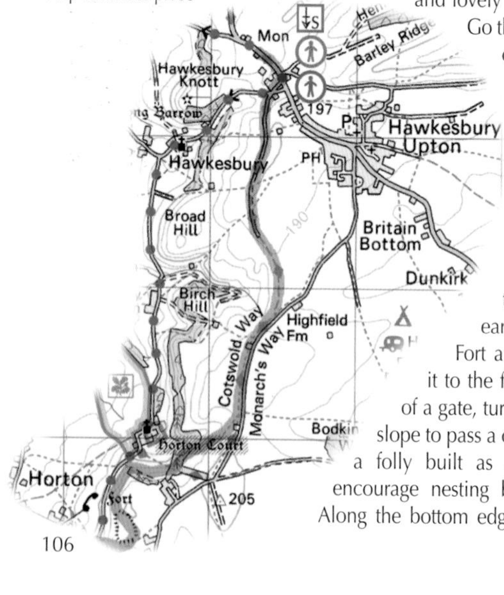

HORTON COURT

This must be one of the oldest inhabited houses in England, for parts in use today were built in 1140, less than 80 years after the Normans arrived. The Norman hall and a detached ambulatory (Italian-style loggia) are open to the public by the National Trust on set days between April and October. The manor was originally in the hands of a son of King Harold. The hall is all that remains of the original construction, but the roof is 14th century. In 1521 the main part of the house was built for William Knight, chief secretary to Henry VIII and the Bishop of Bath and Wells, who was sent to Rome in an attempt to persuade the Pope to annul Henry's marriage to Catherine of Aragon. The attempt was unsuccessful, but Knight had seen much to interest him in Italy, and his attraction to the architecture of Rome was later recreated in parts of Horton Court. St James's Church stands nearby.

Horton Court, one of England's oldest houses

keep ahead to a kissing gate, through which you bear left down to a second kissing gate, where you come onto a road beside the village school a few paces from a junction in the centre of Horton (accommodation).

At the junction bear right, and a few metres later turn left along a drive with a signpost to Little Sodbury. A footpath extends from the drive, crosses through the middle of a field to a stile on the far side, then goes steeply down into a dip with a farm reservoir seen ahead to the left. Go up the opposite slope and into the next field where you trace the right-hand boundary.

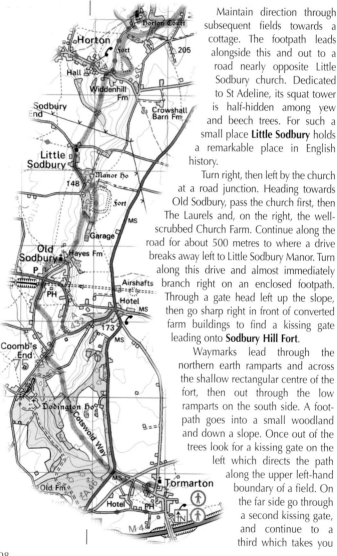

Maintain direction through subsequent fields towards a cottage. The footpath leads alongside this and out to a road nearly opposite Little Sodbury church. Dedicated to St Adeline, its squat tower is half-hidden among yew and beech trees. For such a small place **Little Sodbury** holds a remarkable place in English history.

Turn right, then left by the church at a road junction. Heading towards Old Sodbury, pass the church first, then The Laurels and, on the right, the well-scrubbed Church Farm. Continue along the road for about 500 metres to where a drive breaks away left to Little Sodbury Manor. Turn along this drive and almost immediately branch right on an enclosed footpath. Through a gate head left up the slope, then go sharp right in front of converted farm buildings to find a kissing gate leading onto **Sodbury Hill Fort**.

Waymarks lead through the northern earth ramparts and across the shallow rectangular centre of the fort, then out through the low ramparts on the south side. A footpath goes into a small woodland and down a slope. Once out of the trees look for a kissing gate on the left which directs the path along the upper left-hand boundary of a field. On the far side go through a second kissing gate, and continue to a third which takes you

LITTLE SODBURY

Little Sodbury is a tiny hamlet with a manor built in 1486 for Sir John Walsh. In 1521 William Tyndale came here as chaplain to Sir John's household. He began translating into English Erasmus's *Enchiridion Militis Christiani*, and preaching in what was then seen to be an outspoken manner. One oft-quoted incident occurred when, at dinner one evening at the manor, a visiting dignitary protested at Tyndale's views with the remark, 'We were better be without God's law than the Pope's.' Tyndale was defiant: 'I defy the Pope and all his laws. If God shall spare my life, ere many years I will cause the boy that follows the plough to know more of the Bible than thou doest.'

He left Little Sodbury for London in 1523, then travelled to the continent where he met Miles Coverdale. In 1526 Tyndale's English version of the New Testament was published at Worms, in Germany (the Old Testament followed in 1530), but 10 years later he was put to death. The Parish Church of St Adeline, in which Tyndale preached, originally stood behind the manor, but this was demolished in 1859 and the present church built from some of its stones.

left of Hayes Farm onto an enclosed path. This brings you out by the village school in Old Sodbury.

Walk through the churchyard of the stumpy towered Church of St John the Baptist (the tower is original 13th century), and out at the far side to find a simple topograph erected by villagers to commemorate the start of the third millennium. Views from this sloping meadow extend to the Brecon Beacons. Go down the slope to the bottom left-hand corner and another kissing gate, beyond which you continue towards a black barn with a stile to its left. Walk through the farmyard to the main A432 opposite The Dog Inn in Old Sodbury (grid ref: 754816, accommodation, refreshments).

Cross the road with care, walk along Chapel Lane for about 400 metres, then take a footpath to the left through a kissing gate and go half-right to another kissing gate, beyond which you pass to the left of a small pond, and continue to the far right corner of the field. Maintain direction and climb the hillslope, pass through a gap in a hedge, and continue along the right-hand

SODBURY HILL FORT

Sodbury Hill Fort is one of the most impressive on the walk. Consisting of 11 acres (4½ hectares) enclosed by ramparts and ditches, it was constructed in the Iron Age but considerably strengthened by the Romans who, it is thought, used it as a frontier post. Although never excavated, a few Roman coins have been found in the turf. The Saxon army camped in the shelter of the ramparts in AD577, and in 1471 Edward IV rested here with his army on the way to do battle with Margaret of Anjou at Tewkesbury.

The Cotswold Way cuts through the meadowland heart of Sodbury Hill Fort

side of dividing hedges, making towards the left of some cottages.

Coming onto a country road through a field gate, turn right to Coomb's End. Shortly after passing a road junction the Cotswold Way enters a field on the left, with a sign giving 1½ miles (2.5km) to Tormarton. Walk across the field, passing to the right of a raised group of trees, and on the far side cross a pair of stiles and a long tarmac drive leading to **Dodington House**, unseen off to the right.

The way continues through the parkland, which is often busy with pheasant and guinea fowl. Beside a metal

DODINGTON HOUSE AND PARK

Situated between Old Sodbury and Tormarton, Dodington House is unseen from the Cotswold Way, although it is only a short distance from the path. Occupying the site of a former Tudor house, the rather severe mansion (one of the largest of all in the Cotswolds) was built by James Wyatt in 1795 for Christopher Bethell Codrington, a man whose great wealth was made on the backs of slaves in the West Indies. The rolling parkland was landscaped by Capability Brown 30 years before the house was built, and it is this which brings the Cotswold Way walker another graceful interlude and the company of game birds scurrying to and fro.

Footbridge in Dodington Park

field gate go through a kissing gate, bear half-left, then maintain this direction across Dodington Park by way of a series of stiles and more kissing gates. Eventually cross a footbridge over a stream whose nearby springs are the source of the River Frome, which flows into the Avon at Bristol. Now walk up a gentle slope to the left-hand end of a strip of woodland where the path leads to the busy A46, which has been crossed and recrossed several times since it was first met in Broadway on Section 1.

Cross the road with the utmost caution. The continuing path is signed to Tormarton and begins next to an old milestone half-hidden on the verge. Across the field go over a narrow road and continue straight ahead through the next field with a second lane beyond. Maintain direction through a third field towards a row of houses, but on joining another road bear left and a few paces later turn right to cross a final field towards the Church of St Mary Magdalene. Bear right in front of the church. On coming to a road junction turn left near the Portcullis Inn in the heart of **Tormarton** (grid ref: 768787), which has several possibilities for accommodation, as well as refreshments.

TORMARTON

Tormarton is explored by the route as it makes a dogleg to visit the Church of St Mary Magdalene. Adorned outside by gargoyles, and within by some fine brasses and an interesting Jacobean pulpit, the church is Norman, although it is thought a previous place of worship stood here in Saxon times. In those days the village stood at the borders of Wessex and Mercia, but nowadays the county boundaries of Wiltshire and Gloucestershire are just a short distance away to the east. The national trail now leaves the village by a much-improved route as described in Section 12.

Tormarton church and its table tombs

SECTION 12

Tormarton to Cold Ashton

Distance	6 miles (9½km)
Maps	Harvey's Cotswold Way 1:40,000
	OS Landranger 172 Bristol, Bath & Surrounding
	Area 1:50,000
	OS Explorer 155 Bristol & Bath 1:25,000
Accommodation	Pennsylvania and Cold Ashton
Refreshments	Pennsylvania and Cold Ashton

This very short penultimate stage of the long walk from Chipping Campden is included in order to allow for overnight accommodation before tackling the final 10-mile stretch to Bath. It is an easy stage, with few hills to wander across, but there's more road walking to contend with than on almost any other section. This is not to suggest it is without interest, for the middle part of the walk has Dyrham (and a journey round the perimeter of the 246 acres (100 hectares) of Dyrham Park) as a highlight, and it is near here that a return is made once more to the Cotswold scarp line.

Between Tormarton and Cold Ashton the way goes over the deep cut of the M4 motorway and crosses the A46 yet again. A belt of woodland, followed by a skirting of several large fields, restores the countryside aspect of the walk. Then a country lane takes you to the edge of an extensive deer park surrounding Dyrham House. Ancient field systems (strip lynchets) are seen on the slopes of Hinton Hill, and you gaze across a folding landscape towards Bristol sprawling out to the west. The footpath leads to the edge of lovely, mellow Dyrham, past the gates of Dyrham House, and into fields again on the cross-country route to Cold Ashton, a small village with a marvellous southerly aspect.

Having turned left at the T-junction near the Portcullis Inn, walk out of Tormarton heading south on the grass verge beside the road, and cross the M4 motorway. (Pause for a moment on the bridge and compare your

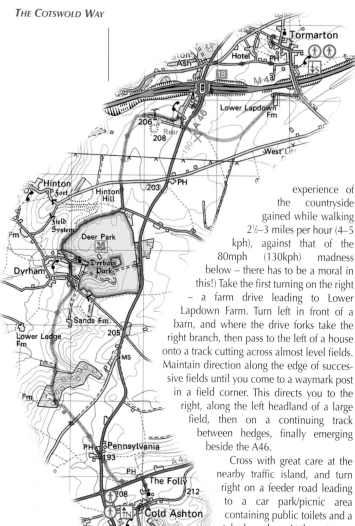

experience of the countryside gained while walking 2½–3 miles per hour (4–5 kph), against that of the 80mph (130kph) madness below – there has to be a moral in this!) Take the first turning on the right – a farm drive leading to Lower Lapdown Farm. Turn left in front of a barn, and where the drive forks take the right branch, then pass to the left of a house onto a track cutting across almost level fields. Maintain direction along the edge of successive fields until you come to a waymark post in a field corner. This directs you to the right, along the left headland of a large field, then on a continuing track between hedges, finally emerging beside the A46.

Cross with great care at the nearby traffic island, and turn right on a feeder road leading to a car park/picnic area containing public toilets and a telephone box. At the entrance to the car park/picnic area take a footpath left into a strip of woodland. Out of this turn left, follow the field boundary beside the continuing woods and you will soon gain a view of folding hills and neat meadows – a welcome return to countryside sanity after the traffic madness of the M4 and A46.

When the woods finish, continue along the field boundary, but near the bottom look out for a waymark

DYRHAM PARK

Dyrham Park consists of 264 acres (107 hectares) of deer-grazed grassland, and the herd of fallow deer is reckoned to be one of the oldest in the country. (Dyrham comes from 'deor ham', meaning deer enclosure, and was thus mentioned in a document of AD577.) The grounds, which surround the imposing Dyrham House, were formerly terraced and landscaped with magnificent water gardens featuring a great water spout and a cascade pouring over a series of more than 200 steps. The house itself, built for William III's secretary of war, William Blathwayt, is in fact two houses standing back to back to replace an original Tudor mansion. The older of the houses was built at the end of the 17th century, the other about six years later (finished around 1704). Now in the care of the National Trust, the house is open on set days of the week between April and November, while the park is open throughout the year.

The path skirts the drystone wall surrounding Dyrham Park

directing the path left into a new field. Walk alongside its right-hand hedgerow and maintain direction on a die-straight course, passing beneath high-voltage power cables as you do, to come to a country road by a T-junction (grid ref: 748769). Take the forward road, Field Lane, to maintain direction, heading towards some barns on the edge of **Dyrham Park**, but immediately before reaching these turn right along a bridleway beside the sturdy grey wall that contains the unseen deer park.

As you walk alongside the wall, note the clear evidence of an ancient agriculture in the low banks of former terracing known as strip lynchets, and the mounded remains of a hill fort above them to the right (north) marked by a woodland: this is **Hinton Hill Fort**. Broad panoramic views produce a tranquil scene all along this part of the walk.

HINTON HILL FORT

Hinton Hill fort is also known as Dyrham (or Burrill) Camp. In AD577 an historic and decisive battle was fought here between the Saxons and the ancient Britons. The outcome gave control of Gloucester, Cirencester and Bath to the Saxons, with the Britons being driven back to Wales and Somerset. An Anglo-Saxon chronicle records the event in concise terms:

> Cuthwine and Cealwin fought against the Brytwalas. They slew three kings, Coinmail, Condidan and Farinmail, at the place called Dyrham, and captured three cities, Gloucester, Cirencester and Bath.

In many ways this battle set the course of English history by re-drawing political and cultural boundaries.

Having wandered round the outside of Dyrham Park, pass through a metal field gate onto a sunken track which takes you down to the modest little village of Dyrham itself, with its mellow stone cottages and bower of trees. Turn left along the village street, passing the entrance to the 13th-century St Peter's Church on your left, closely followed by a set of gates through which can be seen the west side of Dyrham House.

Dyrham House, an imposing mansion now cared for by the National Trust

Shortly after passing the gates you come to a minor road junction. Bear left to rise out of the village, and when you come to the village sign leave the road and head to the right on a signed footpath (Pennsylvania 1½, Cold Ashton 2¼). Walk ahead along the right-hand boundary of a field, go through a kissing gate into a narrow, tree-crowded corner, and then into the meadow beyond.

Maintain direction across the meadow, and through another kissing gate pass alongside a pond, then rise through the centre of a field. Over the brow of the hill a track breaks to the right. Ignore this and continue ahead, now sloping downhill towards trees among which you cross a footbridge over a stream.

Walk across the lower corner of the next field, then up the slope alongside Dyrham Wood. On reaching the top corner the path goes into the wood and eases a way through. ▸

Emerging from Dyrham Wood, walk along a track which leads directly to Gorse Lane. Take care as you cross, for traffic races along here. On the opposite side enter a field and turn left to walk parallel with the road. Go through a kissing gate in the corner then turn right on a bridleway. This keeps to the right-hand edge of another field, at the end of which you maintain direction between hedges and

Note that as you pass a small spring, there's a box on a post beside the path. This contains a 'message book' which encourages walkers to record their impressions of and comments about the Cotswold Way.

117

come to the A46 yet again at the hamlet of Pennsylvania (accommodation, refreshments, grid ref: 744733).

Cross the road with due caution to steps leading into a field on the eastern side. A path cuts diagonally through the field to its top right-hand corner where you go over a stone stile and half-left through a second field to exit onto the A420. Turn left towards the White Hart, then almost directly opposite the pub you follow a footpath alongside a driveway to Holy Trinity Church (grid ref: 751727). Walk through the churchyard, and emerging on its south side bear right on **Cold Ashton** village street. You will pass several handsome buildings gazing out over a magnificent, broad and undulating landscape that folds into St Catherine's Valley, into which the **Limestone Link Path** drops from the road. There's accommodation to be had here in Cold Ashton.

COLD ASHTON

Cold Ashton deserves its prefix by virtue of the winds that sweep in off the Bristol Channel to catch its exposed face. But it is a charming place for all that, perched on the southern edge of the Cotswold plateau with fine views that overlook land on which medieval farmers grew vines. The gabled Elizabethan manor, with its tall chimneys and ornate gateway, stands next door to the rectory, but is partially hidden from the Cotswold wayfarer by walls and clipped yew hedges. Considered to be one of the finest examples of this type of building in the country, it was in Cold Ashton Manor that Sir Bevil Granville died on the night of 5 July 1643 following the Battle of Lansdown in the Civil War (see Section 13).

LIMESTONE LINK PATH

The Limestone Link Path begins in Cold Ashton and journeys for 36 miles (58km) through St Catherine's Valley. It goes alongside the Kennet and Avon Canal to Dundas Aqueduct, then on to the Mendips, where it joins the West Mendip Way. Study of the map shows that this could make a worthwhile alternative route down to Bath; the scenic quality is high, but several historic sites visited by the official Cotswold Way would be missed.

SECTION 13

Cold Ashton to Bath

Distance	10 miles (16km)
Maps	Harvey's Cotswold Way 1:40,000
	OS Landranger 172 Bristol, Bath & Surrounding
	Area 1:50,000
	OS Explorer 155 Bristol & Bath 1:25,000
Accommodation	Bath
Refreshments	Weston and Bath

There are many pleasures to be gained on this final walk: broad panoramas, a varied landscape of hill and low-lying valley, secretive corners – and one of the loveliest vistas to be sampled anywhere along the Cotswolds, just before the last downhill swoop to Bath. Then, of course, there's the architectural climax of Bath itself, best enjoyed perhaps on a late afternoon as the low sun picks out the texture of the town's graceful streets glowing in the westerly light. The last few paces, when you finally turn a corner to face the magnificent abbey directly ahead, and the ancient Roman baths to one side, makes the ultimate finalé to a long distance walk – a truly memorable conclusion to a memorable journey.

Out of Cold Ashton the way makes its final crossing of the A46 and heads along Greenway Lane, which offers as tranquil and pastoral a scene as you could wish for. You then walk through that pastoral landscape and up onto a hilltop called the Battlefields, where there stands a monument to Sir Bevil Granville, killed in the Battle of Lansdown during the Civil War in 1643. The route then goes to the scarp edge at Hanging Hill, across a golf course and along the edge of Bath Racecourse to Prospect Stile. Here there is an uplifting panorama worth savouring, because it's virtually all downhill from now on, round the flanks of Kelston Round Hill, via Penn Hill and the suburbs of Weston, to the elegant streets and gardens of historic Bath.

Continue through Cold Ashton heading west, then slope down to cross the A46 for the last time. On the opposite

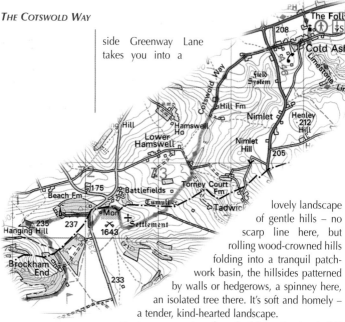

Map continues p.122

side Greenway Lane takes you into a lovely landscape of gentle hills – no scarp line here, but rolling wood-crowned hills folding into a tranquil patchwork basin, the hillsides patterned by walls or hedgerows, a spinney here, an isolated tree there. It's soft and homely – a tender, kind-hearted landscape.

Passing one or two farm buildings the lane's fall steepens and it becomes more narrow, before going through a gateway signed Vale Court Farm. At the foot of the hill the lane curves sharply left. This is where you leave it to go ahead through a wooded corner, then through a kissing gate into a field. Follow the left-hand boundary hedge until it cuts away, then maintain direction across the field above a large pond. Pass through a gateway and continue over the next two fields towards a barn. On reaching the barn at Lilliput Farm turn left along a narrow lane, or track (grid ref: 734710).

The track forks and you take the right branch over a cattlegrid. In a dip there's a second cattlegrid and a stream ford. Now ascend the right-hand hillside, bearing half-right, where two steeply sloping fields linked by a stile bring you to a flattish hilltop field. Walk ahead over this to a kissing gate giving onto a track. Bear right along this track, and when it ends go through a gate and keep ahead along the edge of a sloping meadow. Near the top right-

GRANVILLE MONUMENT

The Granville Monument marks an area known as the Battlefields on Lansdown Hill where, on 5 July 1643, Royalist troops pursued a Parliamentarian army led by Sir William Waller into what became remembered as the Battle of Lansdown. During the pursuit up the hill, Waller's men fired their cannon into the Royalists, but Sir Bevil Granville stormed the hill on horseback in an attempt to stop the guns. He was successful, causing the Parliamentarians to retreat, but at the moment his Cornishmen broke through, Granville was hit and mortally wounded. He was carried to Cold Ashton Manor where he died the same night. The monument was erected in 1720 by Sir Bevil's grandson, Lord Lansdown.

hand corner you'll find a stone stile in a wall, together with a white commemorative stone and an illustrated board giving details of the Battle of Lansdown which took place here in 1643. (There is a very fine view to the south-east.)

Cross the stile and walk along the right-hand side of the battlefield beside the wall. When the wall ends, slant away half-right on a narrow footpath into a small woodland, alongside a low mossy wall, then over a stile to the **Granville Monument** – a fussy memorial surrounded by iron railings (grid ref: 722704).

The Cotswold Way between Greenway Lane and Lansdown Hill

Beyond the monument walk across the meadow to exit onto a road at a parking area where there are two more Battle of Lansdown information panels. Cross half-right to a screen of trees through which you join a narrow service road and turn right.

When the road curves left, go through a gate on the right and follow a grass path parallel with the road heading towards a tall aerial mast. Through another gate by the entrance to the Avon Fire Brigade complex, walk along a narrow lane to the right of the perimeter fence. The continuing footpath breaks half-left ahead, and beyond the fence goes through a gate where you walk along the top edge of a sloping meadow. Once more the way has returned to the scarp edge to regain broad views

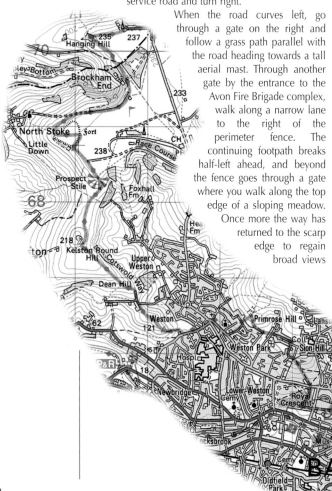

of sweeping hills and lowlands picked out with farms and villages.

At the western end of the promontory of Hanging Hill there's another Battle of Lansdown explanatory panel. Here you go through a kissing gate, pass a trig point and walk along the scarp edge heading south-east. Views once again are magnificent.

The path leads to a golf course where you hug the right-hand wall, and in a few paces drop to a stony drive and bear left. Follow the track as it curves to the right with a woodland on your left. When you come to the end of the wood, head to the right on another track to pass a low building and arrive at a crossing track. Bear left, then right, to walk along the right-hand edge of the continuing golf course alongside Pipley Wood.

Leave the golf course by way of a metal gate and go straight ahead on the continuing track, sloping gently down towards that graceful panorama. After about 120 metres leave the track to rise half-left towards a field gate. Go through the kissing gate beside it into what is at first a fairly narrow meadow, but which begins to open out with yet more big views to enjoy. Stay high as you wind leftwards (heading east), then up a slope onto a hilltop field surrounded by the low earth ramparts of **Little Down Hill Fort**. This is the last of many such Iron Age sites visited since leaving Chipping Campden.

LITTLE DOWN HILL FORT

The most westerly point on the Cotswold Way, this is an Iron Age site of about 15 acres (6 hectares) with a rampart and single ditch still easily identified.

Across the field bear right along the grassy rampart. On reaching a wall the path curves left along the scarp edge again, with views through the trees down to the River Avon, then it brings you to Bath Racecourse. Continue along the scarp to a topograph at a

Kelston Round Hill

prominent vantage point known as Prospect Stile, from where you look into the great bowl of countryside in which Bath lies nestling among hills that seem to gather in an amphitheatre, as if to hold it in an embrace. As this is the first view of Bath, with it comes the knowledge that the long walk is nearing its close. But Bath is not the only object worth gazing on from Prospect Stile; a much better focus is tree-crowned Kelston Round Hill to the south, and out to the west where a huge expanse of low-lying land is invariably patched with cloud-shadows. You gaze down to meadows and trees 600ft (180m) below, and out to a watery dazzle of light. This is a place on which to linger, for the view from Prospect Stile is one to savour (grid ref: 713683).

Go through the kissing gate, bear left, then right through a deer fence to slope downhill along the edge of a plantation. Out of the deer fence turn left on a track, then right along a clear, well-made bridleway heading towards Kelston Round Hill. The way skirts the left-hand (eastern) slopes of this prominent hill with yet more fine views to enjoy as you descend to the head of a lane at Pendean Farm (grid ref: 718667)

A few paces down this lane, take the continuing footpath on the right which cuts along the top edge of a sloping meadow. A stile in the far corner leads onto a path which takes you steeply down to a playing field on the edge of Weston. Cross to the far right-hand corner where you exit onto Anchor Road, and wander downhill.

At the bottom of Anchor Road cross over to the lower street level (High Street), then walk up onto raised Church Street which you follow to Weston's parish church. Go through the churchyard to Church Road and turn left, now walking uphill. At the very top a tarmac path continues to a crossing road, Purlewent Drive.

Cross this and make your way up a narrow service road opposite, which leads to Primrose Hill Water Treatment Works. A footpath continues uphill, through a kissing gate, and turns right along the lower edge of a meadow. On the far side come onto a track which takes you behind houses, then on an enclosed footpath to cross Primrose Hill, a residential street. Continue uphill on a steep tarmac path eased with steps and a handrail, at the top of which you enter Summerhill Road.

Leave this by turning right into narrow Sion Hill, then follow this road as it curves leftwards and brings you to the High Common and a footpath on the right enclosed by iron railings sloping downhill beside a golf course. At the bottom cross Weston Road and walk down the left-hand edge of the Royal Victoria Park. At the bottom take the street to the left which leads past the Victoria Monument.

Beyond the monument bear left on a crossing road, then right on a tarmac path with the curving Royal Crescent seen just above across the neatly trimmed greensward. On a crossing tarmac path go left, then turn right along Brock Street. This takes you to The Circus, a

Bath of course has plenty of accommodation, refreshments, shops, post offices, British Rail, and so on. For tourist information turn right by the abbey entrance – the tourist office is just across the square.

tight circle of houses which you skirt to the right and exit at the first opportunity into Gay Street. Walk down this to Queen Square, turn left into Wood Street which leads into Quiet Street. From Quiet Street bear right into Burton Street, walk straight ahead along Union Street and into elegant Stall Street, along which you turn left to see Bath Abbey facing you and the Pump Room and Roman baths on the right. As the finest of many fine buildings in **Bath**, the abbey is a sight to remember, and a fitting climax to a long and lovely walk. ◄

Congratulations, you've just completed the Cotswold Way!

BATH

Bath was known to the Romans as *Aquae Sulis* – the waters of the sun – and it was these waters that brought the city its fame. They rise at a constant temperature of 120°F (50°C), at a flow of around 250,000 gallons (1,136,500 litres) per day. The Romans were here for 400 years, but after them the Saxons found the place 'a ghostly ruin'. They rebuilt the town, founded an abbey, and in AD973 Dunstan, Archbishop of Canterbury, crowned the first King of all England here. The magnificent abbey seen today, resplendent with carvings and fan-vaulted ceilings, was begun in the 15th century to replace an even larger Norman cathedral.

Modern Bath, of course, has more to offer than the fame gained by exploitation of its waters. It is one of the most architecturally satisfying of all English cities: the elegant showpiece symmetry of the Royal Crescent, the Circus, Queen Square and Lansdown Crescent (built of cream-coloured local stone) all come from the 18th century, after Queen Anne had set the fashion and Beau Nash had made Bath the social heart of the country. If the social aspect of taking the waters has long since vanished, Bath has perhaps gained in the overall charm of the heritage that remains. That heritage is of the Romans, the spirit that lies behind the glory of its abbey, and the architectural genius of the Regency period. Also, of course, it is the local geological heritage that gives Bath in particular – and the Cotswolds in general – a stone that has bequeathed to this part of Britain a unique and endearing character. Tourist information: Abbey Chambers, Abbey Churchyard, Bath ☎0906 711 2000 – calls cost 50p per minute.

Bath Abbey towers over the Roman baths

Bath Abbey, where the long walk north begins

INTRODUCTION

Walking northward along the Cotswold escarpment has certain advantages and no shortage of advocates. For one thing the prevailing weather is at the walker's back (but then so is the sun), and some of the finest views are to be seen when approaching from the direction of Bath. The route becomes more rural the further north you go, and with it you gain a gentle introduction to the essential qualities of the region. This means that, in many ways, one steadily develops over the ensuing miles a deep awareness of the intrinsic nature of the Cotswolds – both countryside and habitation.

From Bath the route climbs onto Lansdown's broad-vista'd escarpment, visits the first of many Iron Age hill forts, crosses a golf course and the site of a decisive Civil War battle, then goes through a lovely bowl of folding hills to reach Cold Ashton. Between Cold Ashton and Tormarton there's a knot of major roads, but these are soon left behind and traded for the peace of Dodington Park where Capability Brown's handiwork becomes the very tapestry of the walker's landscape. Old Sodbury leads by way of another great Iron Age site to Little Sodbury, and from there to Horton on an easy course over low-lying fields. However, near historic Horton Court the way takes you up to a high plateau with hinted views through the trees and a long green track to Hawkesbury Upton.

Between Prospect Stile and Pendean Farm a bridleway provides a hint of Bath below in its basin of hills (Section 1)

Passing the tall monument tower built in memory of one of Wellington's generals, the route now drops into a soft valley to be accompanied for a while by a clear millstream. Alderley is the first 'real' Cotswold village to be discovered on a day that ends in the one- time wool town of Wotton-under-Edge. A steep climb out of town takes you back onto the wolds, emerging from woodlands to be confronted by another lofty monument, this one on Nibley Knoll in honour of William Tyndale, who translated the Bible into English during the 16th century.

Just before reaching Dursley the Cotswold Way makes a tour of Stinchcombe Hill where huge panoramas are a tease of what is to come further north. Then out of Dursley another steep climb takes the way over the outlier of Cam Long Down, and onto the scarp again with opportunities to visit the Uleybury hill fort and Hetty Pegler's Tump. Past yet another ancient site, the route enters woodlands before dropping to Middleyard near the industrial belt spilling out from Stroud.

The stage that journeys from Middleyard to Painswick is utterly delightful – huge views over the Severn and the Vale of Gloucester draw the eye with pleasure, before you drop into a green valley lit by the white-stoned charm of a small town with fine buildings and a memorable churchyard. On then to Birdlip, through more charming countryside, woods with viewpoints to dream over, and beyond Birdlip by way of yet more historic sites and photogenic vistas to the literal high point of the walk on Cleeve Common above Cheltenham.

By now the character of the Cotswolds has become well established, but in many ways the best is yet to come. The route to Winchcombe shows the finest Neolithic long barrow actually on the way (Belas Knap), passes the site of a Roman villa and magnificent Sudeley Castle, then enters an historic little town where the many houses along the main street show what grace of form can be achieved with the use of local stone.

More history waits to be unravelled between Winchcombe and Stanton, while Stanton itself is one of the unrivalled gems of the whole walk – a village of near perfection set in a warm, honey-coloured stone. From there a final 10 mile (16km) stage takes in such viewpoints as those from Broadway Tower and Dover's Hill, a brief exploration of the overly popular village of Broadway, and a wonderful finalé through the streets of elegant Chipping Campden to complete 102 miles (164km) of splendour.

SECTION 1

Bath to Cold Ashton

Distance	10 miles (16km)
Maps	Harvey's Cotswold Way 1:40,000
	OS Landranger 172 Bristol, Bath & Surrounding Area 1:50,000
	OS Explorer 155 Bristol & Bath 1:25,000
Accommodation	Cold Ashton
Refreshments	Weston and Cold Ashton

From the glorious abbey in the heart of Roman Bath to a small village gazing south onto a quiet agricultural landscape, this first stage of the walk offers a variety of scenic pleasures. There are broad panoramas, secretive dales and sites of historic interest to set you in your stride, and once the built-up areas of Bath and Weston have been left behind, waymarking is very good and remains so (with one or two minor exceptions), not only as far as Cold Ashton, but on every section of the walk to Chipping Campden.

The architectural delights of Regency Bath lead to workaday Weston, and from there on a long, and at times, steepish haul to the lip of the escarpment where, if you pause to gaze back, a wonderful view rewards your efforts. Over an Iron Age hill fort, round the perimeter of a golf course and along the scarp edge, the way leads on to the Granville Monument in an area known as the Battlefields, the site of the Civil War's 1643 Battle of Lansdown. Then it's down into a bowl of meadows and fields, followed by hedge-lined Greenway Lane which takes you up the other side, eventually to reach Cold Ashton glowing in its lovely southerly aspect. This final part of the walk, from the Battlefields to Cold Ashton, virtually follows the route taken by Sir Bevil Granville's men when they brought their mortally wounded leader from the hilltop bloodbath to Cold Ashton Manor.

The walk begins by the west door of **Bath**'s finest building, the abbey, which is conveniently reached from Bath Spa railway station. With your back to the abbey,

Please see map, Southbound, Section 13.

and the Roman baths and Pump Room to the left, walk a few paces to find Stall Street and then Burton Street. Turn left to go from Burton Street to Quiet Street, then straight ahead into Wood Street. This leads directly to Queen Square. Head to the right now and walk up Gay Street, which will take you into the Circus, a classic amphitheatre of tightly packed houses all of a style and built around 1754.

BATH

Bath was known by the Romans, who were here for 400 years, as *Aquae Sulis* – the waters of the sun – and it was the hot springs that brought the city its initial fame. However, when the Saxons arrived they found the place 'a ghostly ruin', and set about rebuilding it. It was the Saxons who founded the abbey (subsequently replaced by a Norman cathedral), and in AD973 Dunstan, Archbishop of Canterbury, crowned the first King of all England here. After the magnificent abbey and nearby Roman baths, Bath's main interest lies in the architectural splendour of the Regency period. Tourist information: Abbey Chambers, Abbey Churchyard, Bath ☎0906 711 2000 – calls cost 50p per minute.

Bear left round The Circus and leave it by way of Brock Street. At the end of Brock Street turn left down a footpath, then right at the first junction onto Gravel Walk which leads below the Royal Crescent. From the end of Gravel Walk turn left, then right to pass the Victoria Monument. Now bear right on a road alongside the Royal Victoria Park. Cross Weston Road and continue by way of a fenced footpath climbing alongside a golf course. Emerge from this into a street called Sion Hill where you turn left and wander along until you reach Summerhill Road. Go left again and, at the end of Summerhill Road, find a descending alleyway-cum-path, the steepness of which is eased by steps and a handrail.

On coming to a road (Primrose Hill), cross over and continue down another steep enclosed footpath, pass the top of another road, and go along a track to a metal kissing gate. Waymarks take you through a meadow, then through another kissing gate on the left to descend a path among trees alongside Primrose Hill Water Treatment Works. Continue down a short service road to Purlewent Drive, which you cross to an enclosed tarmac footpath leading directly into Church Road. Go through the churchyard of All Saints Church, and emerge into Church Street, in Weston (grid ref: 731664).

Leave Church Street by going half-left to the High Street, over a traffic island and into Anchor Road. Walk uphill until you come to a large playing field on the right. Enter and cross this, walking more or less parallel with the road, to find a kissing gate leading out of the other side. Ascend the steep grass slope ahead, then veer right to locate the trig point on Penn Hill, the first countryside hill of the walk.

Continue ahead and follow the right-hand hedge to a stile. Keep along the top edge of a sloping meadow as far as a lane by Pendean Farm, and in a few paces the way turns along a bridleway on the right. Rising up Dean Hill, the good clear bridleway then curves round the eastern slopes of Kelston Round Hill, a lovely summit crowned with trees, soon to be seen to full advantage from Prospect Stile.

A bridleway takes the route round the east flank of Kelston Round Hill

North of Kelston Round Hill the bridleway route brings you to a track where you turn left, then right through a deer fence into a plantation. Walk up the slope where you leave the deer fence and soon go through a kissing gate to the topograph at Prospect Stile (grid ref: 713683), where you should pause to contemplate the magnificent view behind you. This is one of the great views of the Cotswold Way. Savour it as you catch your breath.

Bear left along the edge of the escarpment and cross the end of Bath Racecourse. Over this continue ahead and, on coming to the ditch and rampart of **Little Down Hill Fort**, the way curves right and soon after goes to the left to wander through the central part of the fort across a field. On the western side descend a short slope (splendid views ahead), then curve right to a kissing gate next to a field gate. Soon after come onto a track rising gently to a metal gate, through which you enter Lansdown Golf Course alongside Pipley Wood.

LITTLE DOWN HILL FORT

The hill fort marks the most westerly point on the Cotswold Way. This is an Iron Age site covering some 15 acres (6 hectares). The low earth ramparts and single protective ditch are easily identified.

Continue ahead along the edge of the golf course, then over a cross-track to pass a low building on your right (where the wood curves leftwards), and come to another junction of tracks. Turn left and walk along the left-hand side of another woodland. Eventually the track veers left and descends towards a gate. Now head to the right, pass through a gap in a wall and shortly after leave the golf course to follow the wall along the edge of the escarpment once more.

Reaching a trig point on the promontory of Hanging Hill, go through a kissing gate and turn right. Keeping to the top edge of a sloping meadow, walk on to find a gate giving access to an enclosed path alongside the perimeter fence of a complex of buildings owned by the Avon Fire Brigade. On coming to an access road, continue ahead a few paces, then through another kissing gate where a faint path runs parallel with the road. At the end of the meadow section go through another kissing gate, and follow the road a short distance until a waymark post directs you left through a screen of trees to a road opposite a parking area.

Cross with care to find two information boards describing the Battle of Lansdown. A path now crosses a meadow to the **Granville Monument** (grid ref: 722704). Beyond the monument find a stile in a low mossy wall on the right, cross it and follow the wall and fence. Walling continues along the edge of the Battlefields, at the end of which you come to a stone stile. There are wonderful views from here, looking down into a generous folding landscape. Cross the stile, descend a path along the top edge of a sloping meadow, go through a gate and continue on a track.

THE GRANVILLE MONUMENT

The Granville Monument stands on Lansdown Hill in an area known as the Battlefields. On the evening of 5 July 1643, during the Civil War, Royalist troops under the command of Sir Bevil Granville pursued a Parliamentarian army in what became known as the Battle of Lansdown. During the pursuit up the hill, the Parliamentarians fired their cannon into the Royalist troops. Inspiring his men, Granville stormed the hill on horseback and silenced the guns. But he was hit as his troops broke through and, mortally wounded, was carried to Cold Ashton Manor where he died later that night. The monument was erected in 1720 by Sir Bevil's grandson, Lord Lansdown.

When you come to a kissing gate on the left, go through this to cross a fairly flat hilltop field, then continue by descending two meadows to a farm track by a ford. Turn left, cross the stream and two cattlegrids, and wander up a slight slope towards a barn by a house. Now head to the right to cross three fields, the third of which overlooks a large pond. At the far side of this last field go

The Granville Monument on Lansdown Hill

through a kissing gate and a spinney to Greenway Lane. Walk uphill along this steep and narrow lane, passing one or two farm buildings. As you stroll up the lane allow your eyes to wander across the bowl of countryside falling behind and to the side of you. It's a lovely gentle landscape, especially when seen on a bright sunny afternoon, with cows in the pastures and birds and rabbits among the hedgerows.

Greenway Lane brings you to the busy A46, a road that will be crossed and recrossed a number of times in the days ahead. On this occasion you cross to the eastern side and walk uphill on a minor road which leads into the village of **Cold Ashton** (grid ref: 751727), where there's accommodation to be had. (For refreshments, see Section 2, which takes you to the White Hart pub, a short walk north of the church.)

COLD ASHTON

Cold Ashton deserves its prefix by virtue of the winds that sweep across its exposed face from the Bristol Channel. Perched on the southern edge of the Cotswold plateau, from which there are splendid views, it has a small church, and a gabled Elizabethan manor with the handsome Old Rectory next door.

Cold Ashton Manor

SECTION 2

Cold Ashton to Tormarton

Distance	6 miles (9½km)
Maps	Harvey's Cotswold Way 1:40,000
	OS Landranger 172 Bristol, Bath & Surrounding Area 1:50,000
	OS Explorer 155 Bristol & Bath 1:25,000
Accommodation	Pennsylvania and Tormarton
Refreshments	Pennsylvania and Tormarton

With only 6 miles (9½km) to cover, this stage could be walked in a morning, but for those with time to spare, a lengthy diversion into the National Trust's Dyrham Park would be worth considering. Elsewhere there's agricultural land and a couple of woods to wander through, before ending with a short spell of road walking.

From Cold Ashton the route goes across fields to the A46 at Pennsylvania, and from there by way of woods and more fields to the edge of Dyrham village. The route does not actually pass through Dyrham Park, so if this is on your itinerary you'll have to make a diversion of a mile (1½km) to the official entrance beside the A46. Unless, that is, you're a member of the National Trust, in which case it's permissible to enter via the churchyard.

The way passes round the outside of the perimeter wall, with fine views to enjoy and as clear an indication of long-past cultivation, in the form of strip lynchets, as you're likely to see anywhere in the Cotswolds. Near Hinton Hill you pass in view of an historic site where, in AD 577, the ancient Britons fought the Saxons and lost, thereby giving the Saxons control of Gloucester, Cirencester and Bath. Finally, a series of fields brings you to more woods through which you emerge to cross the A46 again, then by way of farmland to another road which takes you across the M4 on the way into Tormarton.

See map, Southbound, Section 12.

Wander through Cold Ashton, with the manor and the Old Rectory side by side on the left, and lovely views of

St Catherine's Valley off to the right, into which the **Limestone Link Path** descends. Bear left into the churchyard and out of the other side, then continue ahead alongside a drive to reach the A420 opposite the White Hart. Cross to the pub and head left alongside the road until you come to a Cotswold Way signpost directing you into a field on the right. Go diagonally across this and the field beyond where, in the far corner, steps lead up to the busy A46 on the edge of the hamlet of Pennsylvania (grid ref: 744733), where there's the possibility of accommodation and refreshments.

LIMESTONE LINK PATH

As its name might suggest, the Limestone Link Path connects the Cotswold Way at Cold Ashton with the West Mendip Way, 36 miles (58km) later. Descending St Catherine's Valley below Cold Ashton, it then follows the Kennet and Avon Canal to Dundas Aqueduct, and continues to the Mendips.

Cross the road with great care onto a driveway opposite. This continues as a bridleway which soon takes you along the left-hand edge of a field. At the far end go through a kissing gate on the left, and walk parallel with a road until you come to another kissing gate giving onto Gorse Lane. Cross to the western side where you walk ahead along a track which takes you into Dyrham Wood. Ignoring a path curving left, wander down the slope through the wood. ▶ Continue through the wood to emerge on the far side into a sloping field with another fine view ahead. Wander down the slope to a woodland shaw and a footbridge over a stream.

Now rise across a hilly field veering a little to the left to join a track beside a hedgerow. Maintain direction alongside the hedgerow to a gap, through which you pass a pond on your right, then come into a field and walk across it to a path tightly enclosed by trees and bushes. Through a kissing gate the path continues ahead, following a hedgerow to a minor road leading into Dyrham village. Turn left on the road, and when you

Note the 'message box' fitted to a post beside a spring. Inside there's a notebook containing comments on and impressions of the Cotswold Way left by other walkers.

The view from Dyrham Wood

come to a junction shortly after, bear right to pass the gateway of Dyrham House on your right.

With the entrance to the church on the right, the road passes some lovely mellow cottages. Opposite these you head off to the right and along a short, sunken track to follow the boundary wall of **Dyrham Park**. As you wander alongside the wall views open out, and before long you will notice a series of strip lynchets (marked as 'field system' on the OS map). Beyond these a clump of trees marks the site of **Hinton Hill Fort** where the Saxons and Britons met in battle in AD577.

DYRHAM PARK

Dyrham Park covers an area of 264 acres (107 hectares), grazed by one of the country's oldest fallow deer herds. Within the grounds lies Dyrham House, an imposing baroque pile built for William III's secretary of war, William Blathwayt, but now in the care of the National Trust. The house is open to the public on set days between April and November; the park itself is open throughout the year.

The wall eventually brings you to Field Lane, where you turn left. On coming to a T-junction, cross ahead and

HINTON HILL FORT

Hinton Hill Fort is also known as Dyrham (or Burrill) Camp. A decisive battle was fought here in AD 577 between the Saxons and ancient Britons, resulting in the Saxons gaining control of Gloucester, Cirencester and Bath, and the Britons being driven back to Wales and Somerset.

maintain direction along the left-hand edge of fields, passing beneath power lines and eventually coming to a gap in the facing boundary hedge. Go through this and turn right along the headland, soon with woods on your right. At the end of the field bear left and continue along its boundary until directed by waymarks into a strip of woodland and out at the other side by a car park and picnic area (with public toilets and telephone box). Bear right on the approach road, so to join the busy A46 at grid ref: 755776.

Cross the road with great care at the nearby traffic island, bear left a few paces, then head to the right on a track between hedges. This leads into a field where you continue ahead to the top corner where there's a CW waymark post. Turn left and follow a die-straight path leading to Lower Lapdown Farm where, after passing a house on your left, you come onto the farm drive. Walk ahead to a barn, then curve right and follow the drive to Marshfield Road. Turn left, cross the M4 motorway, and keep along the road into **Tormarton** (accommodation, refreshments). Just before reaching the Portcullis Inn (grid ref: 767786) take the road on the right which leads to the parish church.

TORMARTON

Tormarton has Saxon origins and a Norman church. Its name means 'the farmstead on the boundary by the thorn-trees'. Standing close to the borders of Wiltshire and Gloucestershire, it shelters among fields a short distance away from the M4 motorway and busy A46.

SECTION 3

Tormarton to Hawkesbury Upton

Distance	8 miles (12½km)
Maps	Harvey's Cotswold Way 1:40,000
	OS Landranger 172 Bristol, Bath & Surrounding Area 1:50,000
	OS Explorer 155 Bristol & Bath, and 167 Thornbury, Dursley & Yate 1:25,000
Accommodation	Old Sodbury, Horton and Hawkesbury Upton
Refreshments	Old Sodbury and Hawkesbury Upton

After the residential streets of Bath and Weston that began the Cotswold Way, followed by the interruption of major roads on Section 2, this part of the walk has a distinctly rural quality to it. There are three or four small villages on the route, and here and there some quiet lanes to wander. But it is the countryside aspect that dominates: the great parkland laid out by Capability Brown, the fields and meadows, the glancing long views, the breezy upland spaces where stone barns hunch their eaves and old trees spread their branches to throw summer shade. There's a large Iron Age hill fort to traverse, and a hamlet nearby where William Tyndale preached more than four centuries ago. It's a peaceful land. Not yet the essential Cotswolds, perhaps, but one senses their drawing power, a hint of good things to come.

Almost as soon as Tormarton has been left behind the way plunges into Dodington Park, where you walk in the shadow of lovely specimen trees and practically trip over pheasant and guinea fowl. Out then to Coomb's End, where field paths make a detour to Old Sodbury. This is soon traded for Little Sodbury, followed by more fields that lead to Horton. Horton Court is an historic place dating from 1140, and from it the way goes uphill, onto a rough plateau to join a former trading route called Bath Lane – a green lane that takes you directly to Hawkesbury Upton.

See map, Southbound, Section 11. There are easy, straightforward road routes out of Tormarton, but the Cotswold Way ignores them and

chooses instead to make a tour of the village. So you turn right (north) at the T-junction near the Portcullis Inn and walk towards the church, then left where a CW sign directs the route across a meadow to a village street. Bear left, then cross into a field on the right beside the Old School House. Now walk ahead across the field, over a narrow road and another field to a second narrow road. A final field crossing is made, on the far side of which you come to the A46 by an old milestone half-hidden among the undergrowth.

Dodington Park, a series of graceful meadows between Tormarton and Old Sodbury

With due caution, cross the road to its western side and through trees come into a meadow. Walk down this to a footbridge spanning the infant River Frome, then follow a path half-left guided by stiles and kissing gates through a series of meadows that form part of Dodington Park. Eventually you will come to the drive leading to **Dodington House** (unseen off to the left). Cross the drive and continue ahead through a field to reach a quiet road at Coomb's End (grid ref: 753805).

DODINGTON HOUSE

Dodington House is one of the largest private houses in the Cotswolds. Unseen from the Cotswold Way, the mansion was built for Christopher Bethell Codrington in 1795 on the site of a former Tudor house, although the great parkland was landscaped by Capability Brown 30 years earlier.

Bear right and walk along the road rising uphill, soon passing a turning to the left. Continue to a cottage beside which you'll see a sign directing you to the left. In the field follow a hedge on your right (northwards), pass through a gap and go down the slope to a kissing gate. Through this, angle across the field aiming half-left towards the far corner, passing a small tree-circled pond as you go. Leave the field through another kissing gate and turn right along Chapel Lane.

Chapel Lane brings you to a junction with the A432 by the side of the Dog Inn at Old Sodbury (grid ref: 754816, accommodation, refreshments). Cross the road with care into a farmyard where, to the right of a black barn, you'll find a stile leading into a field. In the corner half-right across this field, a kissing gate takes you into a sloping meadow. Walk up the slope towards the church, but before you enter the churchyard note the simple topograph and a fine view behind you.

Wander through the churchyard to the lych gate. The village school stands nearby. Take the enclosed footpath next to it which leads past Hayes Farm and into a field. The continuing path goes through more kissing gates and into the top right-hand boundary of a field. There you walk ahead and eventually come onto a path which climbs to the right, up a slope among trees.

At the head of the slope go through a gate on the left, where you enter the earth ramparts of **Sodbury Hill Fort**. Head north across the shallow centre of the fort (now a meadow) and out at the other side. Bear left, go through a kissing gate, then alongside converted farm buildings to a track where you turn sharp left and descend to a country road.

SODBURY HILL FORT

Sodbury Hill Fort is one of the most impressive of its kind on the Cotswold Way. Comprising 11 acres (4½ hectares), it dates from the Iron Age, but was considerably strengthened by the Romans who, it is thought, used it as a frontier post. The Saxon army camped in the shelter of the ramparts in AD577, and in 1471 Edward IV rested here with his army on the way to do battle with Margaret of Anjou at Tewkesbury.

The earth ramparts of Sodbury Hill Fort were constructed during the Iron Age

Bear right. Along the road you will come to a junction by St Adeline's Church in **Little Sodbury** (grid ref: 757833). Turn right, and a few paces later go left beside a cottage, then half-right by the back door into a field. Follow the left-hand boundary hedge and maintain direction through successive fields, passing below a farm reservoir in a dip and up the other side, still in the same direction, then through the middle of a last field, along a short drive, and out to the village street in Horton.

Turn right, and a very short distance later branch left at a junction by the village school on a lane signed to **Horton Court**. ▶ Within a few paces leave the lane to go through a kissing gate on the right, then up a slope to a second kissing gate which takes you into a sloping

Horton Court must be one of England's oldest inhabited buildings, for parts in use today were built in 1180. The Norman hall and a detached ambulatory (Italian-style loggia) are open to the public by the National Trust on set days between April and October.

LITTLE SODBURY

Little Sodbury is a tiny village whose manor was built in 1486 for Sir John Walsh. In 1521 William Tyndale came here as chaplain to Sir John's household, during which time he began to translate into English Erasmus's *Enchiridion Militis Christiani*. He left Little Sodbury for London in 1523, then travelled to the continent where he met Miles Coverdale. Three years later Tyndale's English version of the New Testament was published at Worms, in Germany (the Old Testament followed in 1530), but 10 years later he was put to death. See the Tyndale Monument above North Nibley, visited on Section 5.

Horton Church, a snatched view

meadow. Wander along its lower edge, then angle up towards a stone-built folly erected as a millennium project to encourage nesting swallows and barn owls. Maintain direction beyond the tower and enter Horton Hill Fort. Cut diagonally through this to the far left-hand corner, then walk along the left-hand edge of a hilltop field. The way now enters a belt of trees, through which you descend a zigzag path into a lower field. The continuing path leads to more woodland, which you enter

The way sneaks through a small beech wood above Horton Court

Cotswold view above Horton Court

MONARCH'S WAY

The Monarch's Way is based on the route taken by Charles II after his defeat at the Battle of Worcester in 1651. Beginning in Worcester, the way travels a meandering course to Shoreham, in Sussex, a route of 609 miles (980km). A three-volume guide to the walk has been written by Trevor Antill and is published by Meridian Books.

through a kissing gate. On coming to a path junction cross almost directly ahead and weave among beech trees along the top of the slope, then out through a gate into a scrubby meadow.

After a few paces a marker post directs you half-right, then along the left-hand side of a field. Through a gap in some bushes, pass to the left of a derelict stone barn, and find a kissing gate in a corner. Now walk along the right headland of two fields, keeping parallel with Highfield Lane. At the end of the second field come to a track known as Bath Lane and bear left along it. As far as the Kilcott Valley (Section 4) the route is now shared with that of the **Monarch's Way**. Keep on Bath Lane to its end (about a mile (1½km)), with the tall Somerset Monument glimpsed ahead.

Eventually spill out to a minor road on the northern edge of **Hawkesbury Upton**. Bear right and you will shortly come to a triangle of roads containing a duck pond (grid ref: 775874) – for accommodation or refreshments, turn right; for the continuing Cotswold Way, bear left.

HAWKESBURY UPTON

Hawkesbury Upton began as a farm mentioned in a document of AD972, but the village has grown very little in its thousand-year history. In fact its expansion has been suprisingly limited, considering its prominent position on the wolds just west of the Bath road, and most of its buildings are less than a hundred years old.

SECTION 4

Hawkesbury Upton
to Wotton-under-Edge

Distance	8 miles (12½km)
Maps	Harvey's Cotswold Way 1:40,000
	OS Landranger 172 Bristol, Bath & Surrounding Area 1:50,000
	OS Explorer 167 Thornbury, Dursley & Yate 1:25,000
Accommodation	Kilcott, Alderley and Wotton-under-Edge
Refreshments	None until Wotton-under-Edge

North of Hawkesbury Upton the Cotswold escarpment sends wooded spurs out to the west. Between them millstreams make cheerful companions for valley walks. There are still a few mills left standing beside some of these streams, and on the gentle stroll through the Kilcott Valley we pass one of them. There are woodlands, too, a deeply sunken track cut by centuries of use, and a welcome return to the scarp edge with its big panoramas (the onward route beckoning as you gaze towards tomorrow). And there's Alderley, a small hamlet snug in its warm Cotswold stone, midway between two green valleys. This is a walk of considerable charm, best taken at an easy, unhurried pace.

It begins by passing below the lofty Somerset Monument, erected in 1846 in memory of General Somerset of nearby Badminton, who served under Wellington at the Battle of Waterloo. It then takes to fields and woods before slipping into the Kilcott Valley whose stream is followed north-west for a while. The way now approaches Alderley, then crosses fields to the edge of Wortley before climbing onto the escarpment at Tor Hill. Bridleways, footpaths and a narrow lane take the route from Tor Hill into a final valley for another millstream walk into Wotton-under-Edge.

See map,
Southbound,
Section 10.

At the duckpond in Hawkesbury Upton turn left along the road, and soon reach the tall **Somerset Monument**. Turn right on a drive immediately before the monument,

SOMERSET MONUMENT

The Somerset Monument stands more than 120ft (36m) high, and was erected to the memory of General Lord Somerset, a son of the fifth Duke of Beaufort, after serving under Wellington at the Battle of Waterloo.

The Somerset Monument stands on a hill a short distance from Hawkesbury Upton

and go through a gate by a lodge cottage. Walk ahead along a track across Clay Hill, from which there are long views all around. After about ¾ mile (1km) you come to a junction of tracks on the edge of Claypit Wood. Turn left and walk down the slope to another woodland corner where you take a track cutting into the woods on the right.

On coming out of Claypit Wood maintain direction along the top edge of a field, then swing left through a gateway on a continuing track which bends to the right and takes you down to the Kilcott Valley and a narrow road opposite cottages in the hamlet of Lower Kilcott (grid ref: 787890).

Turn left and walk along the country lane with Kilcott Brook for company for about ¾ mile (1km), passing as you do Kilcott Mill, with its attractive stone buildings and

The village pond, Hawkesbury Upton

millpond on your right. Soon after passing the mill a track breaks away to the right into the Tresham Valley.

The route turns along the track for about 200 metres, then you branch left on an enclosed track-cum-path. Maintain direction along the left-hand edge of several meadows linked by stiles or gates, then along a gently rising farm track into **Alderley**, where you arrive near the village church. Turn right along the road to a junction, where you go straight across into a narrow lane. After a few paces the lane curves right and a path continues ahead to become a track. At the foot of the slope, cross the stream coming from Ozleworth Bottom and go through a gate into a small field. Across this go through another gateway into a larger field where the route aims diagonally across to the top right-hand corner, which brings you to a lane on the outskirts of **Wortley**.

Cross the lane and continue along the farm track opposite. On the edge of a woodland bear right and walk up a sunken track (a magical section of ivy-clung banks and lush fronds of hart's tongue fern) leading onto the escarpment. Once out of the trees continue ahead and keep along the left-hand boundary of fields. Look

ALDERLEY AND WORTLEY

Alderley and Wortley are small neighbouring villages astride a minor road that leads from Hawkesbury Upton to Wotton-under-Edge. 'The clearing in the alders', Alderley is a charming hamlet set on a spur of land between the Ozleworth and Kilcott valleys, and in which the eminent botanist, Brian Houghton Hodgson, lived for a while at The Grange. Worsley was involved in the district's cloth trade by virtue of several mills powered by local streams. Stephen Hopkins made his fortune in that trade and then left Worsley to sail with the Pilgrim Fathers to America in 1620, where he became an important official and died there in 1644.

for the waymark which sends you off to the left through a final strip of woodland, then out onto a terrace of meadowland on the very scarp edge. The path is faint in this grassland, but views are very fine.

Walk across the grassy terrace, and bear right on the far side to follow a wall taking you north-eastward (more splendid views to the left). Keep ahead when you come onto a track and you'll eventually arrive at a narrow road where you head sharp left, now walking a little north of west along Blackquarries Hill. After a little over ½ mile

Cottage in Shinbone Alley, Wotton-under-Edge

(800m), leave the road on a bridleway descending among trees to the right. This brings you to another country road where you turn right and walk into Coombe, but when you come to a millstream, follow this all the way to **Wotton-under-Edge**.

The footpath spills out into Valley Road. Walk ahead along this to Coombe Road, where you bear left and soon reach the Church of St Mary the Virgin. The continuing route leads through the churchyard (grid ref: 760935). The town has a choice of accommodation, refreshments, shops, a post office, and so on.

WOTTON-UNDER-EDGE

Wotton-under-Edge was first mentioned in a charter of AD940. A fire almost completely destroyed the village in the reign of King John, in reprisal for Lord Berkeley's part in the lead up to Magna Carta. Once rebuilt, Wotton became a borough in 1253 and established itself as an important wool town. The oldest building is said to be the former Ram Inn, built to the south of the church in 1350, while there are some attractive 17th-century almshouses in Church Street, with a fine chapel in the courtyard. Tourist information: The Heritage Centre, The Chipping, Wotton-under-Edge ☎01453 521541.

SECTION 5

Wotton-under-Edge to Dursley

Distance	7 miles (11km)
Maps	Harvey's Cotswold Way 1:40,000
	OS Landranger 162 Gloucester & Forest of
	Dean Area 1:50,000
	OS Explorer 167 Thornbury, Dursley & Yate 1:25,000
Accommodation	North Nibley and Dursley
Refreshments	North Nibley and Dursley

Although this may be another short stage, there are two major climbs to be made, the first soon after setting out (leading onto Wotton Hill), and the second on the approach to Dursley with the ascent of Stinchcombe Hill. Both high points give splendid views, as does Nibley Knoll to the north-west of Wotton, where a memorial tower stands as a reminder of the life and work of William Tyndale.

The route passes through Wotton-under-Edge, with the opportunity to study some of its more interesting and attractive buildings, then begins the sharp climb onto Wotton Hill, noted for its circular plantation of trees and striking views. Next, into woods and alongside another Iron Age hill fort, then out to a meadowland on Nibley Knoll, dominated by the Tyndale Monument, before dropping to the village of North Nibley where the last battle in England between private retainer armies took place. A track and two or three field paths make an open approach to Stinchcombe Hill. Last comes the ascent of the scarp slope, followed by a tour round the upper plateau, then descent among woods on the eastern side to the busy little town of Dursley.

Going through the churchyard of St Mary the Virgin, pass the church on your left, walk down an alleyway, then bear right into a second alleyway called The Cloud. Out of this cross to Church Street and walk along it to the end, bearing right into Long Street. Long Street becomes High

Please see map, Southbound, Section 9.

JUBILEE PLANTATION

The Jubilee Plantation on Wotton Hill was initially planted to celebrate Wellington's victory against Napoleon at Waterloo, but in order to mark the end of the Crimean War the trees were felled for a bonfire. The circular wall was erected and more trees planted in 1887 to celebrate Queen Victoria's golden jubilee, and yet more planting took place in 1952.

Street, at the end of which there's a minor crossroads. Go straight ahead into Bradley Street which leads directly to the B4060 at grid ref: 753935.

Bear left and soon you will notice the junction with Old London Road. Just beyond this, cross the road and take the steep path climbing on the right (there are handrails to assist). This path brings you to a narrow lane, across which a set of steps and a kissing gate take you to the foot of a steep meadow. Climb this meadowland slope to the **Jubilee Plantation**, a clump of commemorative trees contained within a circular wall.

Continue to the top left-hand corner of the meadow where another kissing gate leads into a large field beside a woodland. Maintain direction along the left-hand boundary of a large field, then curve left into Westridge Wood. The track forks and meets several alternative paths, but marker posts aid direction-finding. On the way through the wood you pass along the right-hand edge of the somewhat overgrown hill fort site of Brackenbury Ditches. ◀

On emerging from the woods, follow the left-hand fence boundary of the open meadowland of Nibley Knoll, and walk towards the towering **Tyndale Monument** which dominates it. From the base of this rather solemn-looking tower, as from the scarp edge by which you approach it, magnificent views are to be enjoyed on a clear day. A topograph nearby highlights noteworthy places to be seen. (It is possible to climb the tower, but the key must first be obtained from a house in North Nibley below. The key's location is given on a notice-board at the foot of the track which leads down to the

Brackenbury Ditches is the name given to another Iron Age hill fort, now rather overgrown with trees. The outer defensive ditch has been cleared, but the site has never been excavated – possibly because of the dense woodland cover within.

village – although you'd have to be extremely keen to climb all the way back to Nibley Knoll at the end of this stage!)

From the tower head to the right and descend numerous steps through a steep woodland. The steps give onto a track leading out to the B4060 in the village of **North Nibley** (accommodation, refreshments, shop) (grid ref: 741957). Cross the road with care and bear right. Before long come to a junction where you turn left into The Street. Walk along this for a short distance, then break off to the right into Lower House Lane.

The way leads through Westridge Wood between Wotton and North Nibley

TYNDALE MONUMENT

The Tyndale Monument is one of the most prominent man-made features along the Cotswold Way, being visible on the escarpment from a considerable distance. It stands 111ft (34m) high and was erected in 1866 in memory of William Tyndale (1484–1536), who translated the Bible into English and was martyred for his dedication. See also Little Sodbury box, Section 3.

NORTH NIBLEY

North Nibley means 'the clearing near the peak'. Among its oldest dwellings is the large grey Nibley House, which was partially rebuilt in 1763 from an earlier, possibly 17th-century house. Set back from the village, the Church of St Martin is a fine building that dates from the 15th century, while nearby Nibley Green is where the last battle to be fought in England between private armies took place. In 1470 some 2000 men took up arms on behalf of the Berkeleys and the earls of Warwick over ownership of Berkeley Castle. Lord Lisle, who had challenged Lord Berkeley to do battle, was shot in the face then stabbed to death. His retainer army then fled while his house was sacked by Berkeley's men. Around 150 men lost their lives in the fighting.

An enclosed path continues from the lane and becomes almost a tunnel among trees. Along this section of the walk note an old doorway dated 1607 in the left-hand wall. The path finally emerges onto the B4060 again, which you cross straight ahead to walk down a metalled lane. Soon after crossing a stream you come to some cottages and climb out of the lane over a stile on the left. Go up the sloping meadow to a second stile, then across a large field to a narrow road near the entrance to Park Farm House (grid ref: 743972).

A Cotswold Way sign is found to the left of the house, directing you into a hillside meadow. The way now leads through linking meadows, then into woodland where you cross a gully noted for some gas pipes nearby. The continuing route then rises up the wooded scarp face to emerge beside the golf course on **Stinchcombe Hill**.

STINCHCOMBE HILL

Stinchcombe Hill is a high spur of land projecting from the escarpment, with magnificent vantage points from which to study the distant Brecon Beacons, Malvern Hills and Berkeley Castle. A topograph near Drakestone Point highlights some of the salient features in the panorama. The hilltop was given to the public by Sir Stanley Tubbs in 1930, and now houses Dursley Golf Club.

From Drakestone Point on Stinchcombe Hill the view includes the Brecon Beacons and Malvern Hills

SHORTCUT

The Cotswold Way makes a lengthy circuitous tour of the plateau, but should you need to get to Dursley in a hurry, or the weather is poor and visibility such that you won't have the views, it's possible to make a shortcut across Stinchcombe Hill, as follows. On coming to the edge of the golf course, simply walk straight ahead along the right-hand side of a fairway – marker posts guide the way – and very soon you'll come to a narrow road which crosses the golf course. Turn right, then almost immediately go left to reach the clubhouse on whose right-hand side you rejoin the main route.

A large oak signpost directs the route left to make a devious 2 mile (3km) clockwise tour of Stinchcombe Hill. Numerous marker posts lead the way alongside the golf course fairway and in and out of brief woodland sections. At various promontories you gain long views south to Nibley Knoll, west to the Severn and northwest across the Vale of Berkeley. North of Drakestone Point you come to the stone-built Tubbs Shelter, then continue round the wooded fringe of Stinchcombe Hill.

After an open section, the path steers left into woodland, then right near a wooden barn, eventually returning to the edge of the fairway. Marker posts direct the continuing route into more woodland, then out alongside the fairway to a group of barns. Not long after passing these you come to the golf clubhouse, to be met by the alternative shortcut route (see box on page 159).

Beside the clubhouse a path breaks away and descends through woodland to Dursley, which you enter on Hill Road. Continue downhill, curving left at the bottom by The Old Spot pub into May Lane. Coming to a shopping precinct on the right, walk through it as far as the Market House opposite the 15th-century Parish Church of St James in the very heart of **Dursley** (grid ref: 757982). Dursley has a range of accommodation, refreshments, shops, a post office, and so on.

DURSLEY

Dursley was once one of the principal wool and cloth towns of the Cotswolds, but now its dependence on sheep is but a memory. However, the town survives in its own right, and the old Market House (dated 1738) is one of its show-piece buildings. On it there's a bell turret, and a niche containing a statue of Queen Anne facing the parish church.

SECTION 6

Dursley to Middleyard (King's Stanley)

Distance	6½ miles (10½km)
Maps	Harvey's Cotswold Way 1:40,000
	OS Landranger 162 Gloucester & Forest of
	Dean Area 1:50,000
	OS Explorer 167 Thornbury, Dursley & Yate, and
	168 Stroud, Tetbury & Malmesbury 1:25,000
Accommodation	Uley, Middleyard and King's Stanley
Refreshments	None until King's Stanley

The modest distance covered by this section belies the energetic nature of the route. There is much height to be gained and lost – the crossing of a classic outlier, Cam Long Down, and the ascent and re-ascent of the steep scarp face. There are interesting archaeological sites, both on the route and a short distance from it, woodland walks, and yet more extensive views to enjoy.

Out of Dursley one is at first lulled into a sense of ease with a series of meadows and low-lying field paths, but then comes a steep climb up Cam Long Down with a superb view from the top, followed by a sharp descent that leads to the foot of the main scarp face. A sunken track takes you almost to the top of this near the earthworks of Uleybury promontory fort, then a short traverse is made before dropping through trees to the foot of the slope once more. Having reached the low point, you then have to re-ascend once more to Frocester Hill, pass the Nympsfield long barrow, and plunge into woods for a long up and down traverse of the scarp before heading down to Middleyard and King's Stanley, south-west of Stroud. It's a fine walk, constantly interesting, varied and scenic.

From the Market House in Dursley bear left and walk down Long Street, leaving it when the road makes a left turn by a building named The Priory. Veer right here on a lane that becomes a drive leading to The Chestal, a large house at the head of parkland. Coming to this parkland,

Please see map, Southbound, Section 8.

Dursley, backed by Stinchcombe Hill

go through a kissing gate on the left and angle across the meadow (the way was not clearly defined during research) towards its top left-hand corner where you will find a gateway leading into a very small meadow. Across this veer slightly right to enter a larger meadow where you now keep ahead alongside the left-hand boundary. Reaching the far boundary fence go through a metal kissing gate, turn left and follow the fence for about 100 metres, where you then break away to descend through the pasture. The path then accompanies a stream along the edge of linking meadows and behind a cottage garden, before emerging onto a lane nearly opposite farm buildings (grid ref: 771989).

Cross half-right to a sign that directs the continuing route into a sloping meadow. Walk up the slope towards Cam Peak (Peaked Down), and on gaining the top boundary cross a stile and turn right on a crossing path. Branch half-left ahead when the path forks soon after having joined it, and you will come to a multi-junction of paths on the saddle which lies between Cam Peak and

CAM LONG DOWN

Cam Long Down and its slightly lower neighbour, Cam Peak (or Peaked Down as the OS has it), are outliers from the main Cotswold escarpment linked one to another by an obvious saddle. Summit views are far-reaching – among the best of the whole walk – and include another outlying neighbour to the south, Downham Hill. The rough undulations of the summit suggest that it could have been the site of some form of ancient settlement.

Cam Long Down. Take the main path ahead which now ascends grass-and-bracken slopes to the undulating summit crown of **Cam Long Down**.

The summit panorama is impressive. In the west the windings of the River Severn are backed by the Forest of Dean. Below to the south-west lies Dursley, to the south the tree-crowned Downham Hill, while the long curving bow of the Cotswold escarpment stretches away to the north.

Cross the summit ridge to its eastern end, then descend half-right among trees on a path of steps that leads to a stile under an oak tree. Over this continue down the hillside meadow and across a field towards some barns. Now walk ahead along a narrow country lane and when it curves to the right, break away left and follow the farm track leading to Springfield and Hodgecombe Farms (accommodation at the latter). The track goes between the farms to enter Coaley Wood, which it then climbs as a steep, sunken way (sometimes muddy and cut by horses' hooves). It emerges almost at the top of the scarp slope near **Uleybury Hill Fort**. ▸

Note To visit Uleybury simply go up a little further onto the lip of the escarpment. An interesting circuit can then be made of the ramparts of this ancient site.

ULEYBURY HILL FORT

The hill fort occupies more than 30 acres (12 hectares) of land on the very edge of the escarpment south-east of Cam Long Down. Dating from the Iron Age it is certainly a well-chosen site, for it has a 300ft (91m) drop down the scarp face to help protect it. A ditch and earth ramparts complete the defences. Although the site has never been excavated, Roman coins from the second and fourth centuries have been found there.

To continue the Cotswold Way go over a crossing track and take the opposite path to make a traverse of hillside below an exposed quarried cliff. The path now slopes downhill a little then takes a gently undulating course through the woods, carpeted with wild garlic in springtime. At a junction of paths take the upper option through a gate, contour across the hillside, but after passing through more gates you then climb steeply along a stony bridleway to reach the B4066 a short distance from **Hetty Pegler's Tump**, a Neolithic burial chamber.

HETTY PEGLER'S TUMP

Hetty Pegler's Tump lies just off the route of the Cotswold Way. Measuring 140ft long by 90ft wide (42m x 27m), this Neolithic long barrow has a covering mound of about 10ft (3m). Accessed from a long internal passageway, there are two pairs of side chambers and a single chamber at its western end; the two northern chambers have been sealed off. Excavations in the 19th century unearthed pieces of Roman pottery and an Edward IV silver groat. The mound (or tump) gained its curious name from the 17th-century owners of the land, Henry and Hester (or Hetty) Pegler.

Note If you wish to visit Hetty Pegler's Tump – or Uley Tumulus, as it is also known – turn right and walk along the road for about ½ mile (800m). A key is available at Crawley Barns to enable visitors to enter the main chamber.

◄ Bear left alongside the wood, then left again at a junction onto a road descending Frocester Hill. A few paces along this turn right on a woodland path, go down some steps and past a quarried cliff. Continue along the path, which eventually emerges from trees and scrub through a kissing gate, and rises onto a green hilltop meadow at Frocester Hill, with yet more splendid views – especially towards Cam Long Down and Cam Peak. Wander along the scarp edge to pass **Nympsfield Long Barrow** (grid ref: 794015) with the car park of Coaley Peak Country Park to your right.

Cross the meadowland beyond the long barrow and be guided by waymarks into woodland again. The path takes you alongside a small fenced quarry with the road not far off to the right. You then bear left on a waymarked path which begins the descent of the slope. There are several crossing tracks and alternative paths, but

NYMPSFIELD LONG BARROW

Nympsfield Long Barrow is similar in concept to many Neolithic barrows of the Severn-Cotswold Group. Constructed around 2800BC it was used for burials and, probably, as a place of ritual. The site was first excavated in the 19th century when the remains of 13 people, together with a flint arrowhead and some pottery, were discovered in the pair of side chambers that lead from the main passageway.

waymarks keep you on course and eventually bring you out of Stanley Wood through a kissing gate above Woodside Lane. Walk along the upper edge of a meadow, pass above Woodside Farm, then cut across the slope a little to find a stile leading into some jungly undergrowth. The path soon improves and rises gently through the mature beech woods of Pen Wood.

ALTERNATIVE ROUTE

While the traditional Cotswold Way leaves Pen Wood at grid ref: 818027 on a path leading to Middleyard and King's Stanley (for accommodation and refreshments), a longer alternative route has been created that avoids these two neighbouring villages.

On the northern edge of Pen Wood a junction of paths is marked by an oak signpost. The main CW path is signed to King's Stanley, but the alternative route goes ahead via Selsley Common to Ryeford (3½ miles). Take the lower of two paths, sloping down to the bottom edge of the woods. It passes two houses, crosses a drive and curves into a bay of the hills. When the path forks, branch right, climb to the eastern edge of the woods and leave by a kissing gate which takes you onto the open slopes of Selsley Common. From the west flank of the Common the Malvern Hills can be seen far ahead, while the River Severn gleams to the left. Remain high, just below the crest of the hills, until the path angles half-left down towards Selsley church.

Come to a road junction (grid ref: 829037), cross ahead and turn right towards Selsley East and Stroud. Beyond the church and neighbouring gothic building of Stanley Park the road forks at Bell Lane. A squeeze stile on the left gives into a sloping meadow (further along the road another path cuts left to join this one). Cross two sections of meadow with the aid of marker posts to show the way, and come to the A419.

Cross by way of pedestrian-controlled traffic lights and turn left on a tarmac path. Take the upper option when the path forks, and soon after descend a flight of wooden steps to a small field near Ebley Mill. Bear left through linking fields alongside the little River Frome. The way eventually takes you across the stream on a bridge, and ahead to the Stroudwater Canal where you turn left. This section of canal ends as you cross a narrow service road and maintain direction through a rather untidy area of scrub and damp patches indicating the canal's one-time course. At an abandoned lock it is met once more, but this is a sad, neglected stretch of algae-covered water that you walk beside as far as a road bridge at Ryeford (grid ref: 813046).

For accommodation at King's Stanley turn left and follow directions on page 81, but for the continuing northbound Cotswold Way turn to page 168.

The path makes a clear traverse through the woods below Pen Hill, then goes down an enclosed path which leaves the woods and comes onto the very narrow Pen Lane. In a few paces enter a field on the right and descend this to an enclosed footpath feeding onto a drive which takes you out to a road in Middleyard by the side of Rosebank Cottage. Cross the road and bear left for about 50 metres to find King's Stanley Baptist Church on the right (grid ref: 820032).

Note The quickest route into King's Stanley for accommodation and/or refreshment is along the road beyond the Baptist Church. The Cotswold Way takes a country route, and doesn't actually enter the village, although it does take you close by where there's a good feeder path. This is described at the start of Section 7.

SECTION 7

Middleyard
(King's Stanley) to Painswick

Distance	9½ miles (15km)
Maps	Harvey's Cotswold Way 1:40,000
	OS Landranger 162 Gloucester & Forest of Dean Area 1:50,000
	OS Explorer 179 Gloucester, Cheltenham & Stroud 1:25,000
Accommodation	King's Stanley, Randwick (+ ½ mile (800m)), Haresfield (+ ¾ mile (1km)), Edge and Painswick
Refreshments	Edge and Painswick

This is one of the loveliest sections of the Cotswold Way. It climbs out of Stroud's industrial valley and onto the escarpment, through woods, out to jutting prows, and gives memorable views over birch-speckled commons with the white stone of Painswick beckoning ahead. Painswick itself makes a happy end to the day: an old market town with interesting backstreets, it also has an utterly delightful churchyard noted far and wide for its neatly trimmed yews and table tombs. Once away from the thunderous traffic descending on Stroud there's barely a dull moment. It's a country walk of considerable variety with many a long mile of nature's own peace.

From Middleyard the way leads across fields to Stanley Mill. There follows a short stretch of road walking, but then you break away and climb a hillside on the western edge of Stroud's probing tentacles, up to high, bird-raucous Standish Wood and out to a pair of promontories with outstanding panoramas. Haresfield Beacon is the second of these, a glorious spot worth savouring. After this, it's back to woods again along the edge of Scottsquar Hill, over Edge Common and a series of meadows, to finish in the bleached delight that is Painswick.

The continuing path nudges down the left-hand side of King's Stanley Baptist Church, through a squeeze stile

See map, South-bound, Section 7.

Note For accommodation and/or refreshments, continue ahead, cross a stream in a wooded gully and emerge to a playing field. King's Stanley village lies on the other side – pubs, shops, a post office, and so on.

and ahead to a fence. In the next field go half-left at the back of garden boundaries to the corner, then along the left-hand hedge of a third field. Another stile takes you into a larger arable field which you cross to a narrow farm drive. Cross directly ahead and walk along the boundary to a kissing gate on the right. ◄

For the continuing Cotswold Way go through the kissing gate and along the side of a garden boundary to a scrub corner. Veer right and soon enter a meadow. Cross to a second meadow whose path eventually comes out on a road a short distance from **Stanley Mill** (grid ref: 813043).

STANLEY MILL

Stanley Mill is a five-storey building constructed from brick and stone in 1811, when its great looms were powered by no less than five water-wheels. These gave way to steam power in 1827. In its heyday Stanley Mill employed almost 1000 workers, but it is now obsolete.

Bear right along the road and soon come to the A419. Cross at the pedestrian traffic lights, turn left and in a few paces bear right into Ryeford Road North. Before long you cross the **Stroudwater Canal** to be joined by the alternative Cotswold Way route which parted company from the main route in Pen Woods.

STROUDWATER CANAL

The canal opened in 1779 to service the industrialised Stroud Valley. It was only 8 miles (12½km) long, but it linked Stroud with the navigable River Severn at Upper Framilode by way of a dozen locks. At the time of writing there are plans to restore the canal, although no date has been given for this.

A little further up the road will bring you to the B4008, which you cross and turn right. Go beneath a footbridge and, a short distance beyond, opposite a garden centre, bear left and walk along the edge of a sports field, over a railway footbridge and into a field where you bear right alongside a hedge. Two more fields linked by stiles are crossed, then you walk alongside another boundary hedge to a stile beside a field gate in a dip. Ascend the meadow beyond, passing beneath power cables as you do, and find a squeeze stile by an oak tree. The path continues in the same direction to a further stile which leads onto a narrow road.

Turn right for about 200 metres, then bear left between houses at Westrip. The way rises through meadows and out to a second narrow road (grid ref: 822060). Turn left, then veer right to enter Three Bears Wood, a short strip of woodland which the path wanders through.

At the top of the wood a stone stile leads out to a meadow. Cross to a gateway on the right and follow the left-hand stone wall. This brings you to a crossway at the head of a narrow lane which leads on the right to Randwick. Walk directly ahead, then veer leftwards on a bridleway entering Standish Wood (grid ref: 824067). This woodland is especially fine in springtime, when you walk among vibrant carpets of bluebells. ▶

The route through Standish Wood is almost 2 miles (3¼km) long, with several crossing tracks and alternative paths that might confuse, had the way not been so well waymarked.

Near Haresfield Beacon on Ring Hill the path skirts the steep scarp slope

At each junction look for the distinctive CW arrow. You will eventually rise out of the wood and into the National Trust's Cripplegate car park. Bear left and wander across an open hilltop spur to find a raised topograph with superb views out to the Vale of Gloucester and the windings of the River Severn glinting in the light.

From the topograph cut back to the right (heading north) to the far left-hand corner of the meadow, where a waymark directs you left onto a broad path descending among trees. After making a short contour the path then regains lost height by climbing again to road level. Without going onto the road, head sharp left on the waymarked path which leads through the earthworks of another hill fort (mostly confused by trees and scrub). The clear path winds leftwards round the promontory and goes directly to the trig point on **Haresfield Beacon** (grid ref: 820088).

HARESFIELD BEACON

The beacon is a splendid promontory viewpoint at the top of Ring Hill, on which there was once an Iron Age hill fort of 10 acres (4 hectares). We know that the Romans were also here, because excavations at the eastern end of the hill in 1837 unearthed traces of a Roman building and a pot containing nearly 3000 coins.

This is one of the finest viewpoints on the Cotswold Way. A huge panorama overlooks the Vale of Gloucester, River Severn, Forest of Dean, and so much more. In spring the hawthorn bushes are afroth with blossom and the grasslands dazzling with wild flowers. In October autumn colours burnish the scene. There's a wondrous sense of space, and this is a great place to spread yourself on the lush turf and allow the long walk to come into perspective; it is a picnic spot *par excellence*.

Return from the trig point spur heading north-east, with the slope falling away to your left. Through a gate follow the path ahead down to Ringhill Farm. Bear left on the lane, then take the track on the right. This leads without confusion through woods, passes Cromwell's Stone (on a bend) and comes out to another quiet lane between Cliffwell Cottages and a well-head in its stone-built housing (grid ref: 833095).

Bear right along the lane for about 350 metres, then leave it to take a bridleway forking left into Halliday's Wood. This track can be rather muddy at times and, in places, heavily threatened by rampant growth on either side. The way follows it for a little over ½ mile (800m), passing an unusual hexagonal house on the left, before coming to a narrow path climbing to the right through Stockend Wood.

On arrival at a minor road near some abandoned quarries on Scottsquar Hill, cross to find a narrow path working its way left of the quarries. Beyond them waymark posts direct you south-eastward down the slopes of Edge Common, with views ahead to Painswick backed by the dark green of woodland. At a major crossing path (or track), continue down the slope and you'll soon reach a gate leading on to the A4173 Gloucester-to-Stroud road opposite the Edgemoor Inn. (The village of Edge lies just a short walk along the road to the left.)

Cross the road with care, turn right along the pavement, then take the first turning left into Jenkin's Lane. Shortly before reaching Jenkin's Farm a sign directs you left through a gate and down some steps into a field. Walk ahead to find a pair of gates either side of a farm track. Through these walk down the meadowland slope, soon coming to an upright stone marker displaying the acorn symbol of a national trail. On one side of the stone it says: 'Chipping Campden 47', on the other 'Bath 55'. Continue down the meadow and into a strip of woodland. Over a footbridge you soon leave the wood near two large barns at Washbrook Farm.

Passing the barns a track curves left to the grey 17th-century farmhouse. Turn right in front of the farm, cross a stream and follow a path alongside trees. Go through a gate and wander across a field to its opposite boundary, then bear left for about 50 metres to a kissing gate in a corner near a tennis court. Continue up the next field to find an enclosed footpath at the back of some houses. This brings you into Hambutts Field (owned by the Open Spaces Society), which you cross along its right-hand edge and emerge into Edge Road. Turn right and walk a short distance to New Street in **Painswick,** opposite the lych gate of the splendid churchyard (grid ref: 866097). Painswick has a good choice of accommodation and refreshments. There's a small supermarket and a post office, and bus links with Cheltenham and Stroud.

PAINSWICK

Painswick is a delightful old market town whose stone is strangely white, or light grey, in colour. As a result the houses appear a little more formal than those to be seen north of here, where the colouring is more honey-gold. However, there's much of interest that will repay more than a cursory glance. Dating from the 13th century, New Street is one of the town's oldest, but other streets – notably those north-east of the church – are also worth exploring. Friday Street indicates the site of the weekly market, while Bisley Street has a collection of splendid old buildings, and at the top of Hale Lane the old town stocks remain.

Like many Cotswold towns, Painswick owes its elegance to the cloth trade, at the height of which 25 mills were being powered by local streams. In the Civil War Royalists attacked the town, damaging St Mary's Church with fire and cannonballs – marks of which are evident to this day. The churchyard is noted for its numerous clipped yew trees, its Renaissance-style table tombs, and the lych gate, whose timbers, decorated with carved bells and music, came from the belfry roof after the spire collapsed in 1883. At 174ft (53m) high, the spire can be seen from a great distance, and the church it advertises is a true gem. Tourist information: Painswick Library, Stroud Road, Painswick ☎01452 813552.

SECTION 8

Painswick to Birdlip

Distance	7 miles (11km)
Maps	Harvey's Cotswold Way 1:40,000
	OS Landranger 163 Cheltenham & Cirencester Area, and 162 Gloucester & Forest of Dean Area 1:50,000
	OS Explorer 179 Gloucester, Cheltenham & Stroud 1:25,000
Accommodation	Cooper's Hill, Little Witcombe (+ 1½ miles (2½km)), and Birdlip
Refreshments	Prinknash, Cooper's Hill and Birdlip

Much of this stage of the walk goes through woodland, but there are open panoramic viewpoints too. The hill fort site of Painswick Beacon gives popular views, as does Cooper's Hill at the head of the famous cheese-rolling slope. Buckholt and Brockworth woods are nature reserves. There is the site of a Roman villa just off the route and also Prinknash Abbey just below the scarp slope.

Away from Painswick's dusky-white buildings the route soon climbs once more onto the wolds near a hamlet charmingly named Paradise. Painswick Beacon tops a trim golf course and the walk takes you alongside it, into Pope's Wood and, skirting the scarp edge, passes above Prinknash Abbey. It then goes through more woodlands and emerges to lovely views on Cooper's Hill. Down then to a string of cottages enjoying the fine views north, before plunging again among trees on the long unbroken woodland stretch to Birdlip.

The straightforward route through Painswick simply follows New Street uphill to the left as far as Gloucester Street, where it turns left. (There is an interesting alternative route, however, that adds very little distance and is worth taking. Go across New Street and through the lych gate into the churchyard with its magnificent yews and

Please see map, Southbound, Section 6.

A snatched Cotswold view through the trees above Paradise, near Painswick

table tombs. Pass the church to your right and exit the churchyard on the far side to find the town's iron stocks. Bear left along St Mary's Street, then fork left into Friday Street. This leads to Bisley Street which takes you left up to New Street again. Cross this directly into Gloucester Street to resume the official way.)

Walk uphill along Gloucester Street, passing the one-way system which directs the B4073 down into town, until you come to a minor road branching right. Walk along this, then on a footpath beside trees until you reach the lower part of a golf course. Aim across this towards the left-hand side of a church and its cemetery. Continue ahead with the cemetery wall on your right, so passing the little church that serves the parish of Paradise. Beyond the wall cross another open golf-course fairway to a clear path heading through a strip of woodland (tree-screened views off to the right). Pass Catsbrain Quarry and go on a track to a narrow lane climbing leftwards uphill across the golf course. A short distance along this lane, break away to the right on a waymarked path. This takes you across the golf course between fairways heading north-east below the crown of **Painswick Beacon** (grid ref: 867121). It's worth making a slight diversion onto the hill for the views.

PAINSWICK BEACON

Painswick Beacon has several other names: Painswick Hill (on the OS map), the Castles, Castle Godwyn and Kimsbury Hill. Overlooking Gloucester and the Severn Vale it was settled as a hill fort by late Iron Age tribes, was used in 1052 as a temporary camp by Earl Godwyn (a Saxon leader in conflict with the Earl of Mercia), and again in 1643 by Royalist forces following the lifting of the Siege of Gloucester. The 250 acres (101 hectares) of common land are speckled with birches and the manicured fairways and greens of Painswick Golf Club.

The route across the golf course is extremely pleasant and relaxing to walk, with no hills to tackle and few alternative trails to confuse. On the far side you

On the outskirts of Painswick the route crosses a golf course below Painswick Beacon

Prinknash Abbey lies down the slope about ½ mile (800m) to the north, where refreshments can be had at the visitor centre.

enter Pope's Wood and join a metalled lane. When this curves right you continue ahead on a clear track. It soon comes to a minor road, which you cross and continue ahead, then veer right alongside the boundary wall of Prinknash Park. After about 100 metres reach a junction of roads at Cranham Corner, also known as Prinknash Corner. ◄

Cross the A46 and walk ahead along Sanatorium Road, then fork left on a path among fine beech woods. Waymarks direct you along the correct path as there are several alternative tracks, some rather enticing. Brockworth and Buckholt woods are linked by a short and well-waymarked 'corridor', and the route continues to wind its way, now among ash, sycamore and birch, as well as the ubiquitous beech, until at last you emerge to an open grassy glade on **Cooper's Hill**, with its maypole at the head of the cheese-rolling slope (grid ref: 892146). Splendid views are enjoyed here, with the Malvern Hills and Black Mountains among the points of interest to be picked out on a clear day.

Descend leftwards through more trees on a curving path that brings you out to a collection of cottages on a narrow lane. Follow the lane to the right, soon to pass a cottage advertising teas and snacks. The Haven Tea

COOPER'S HILL

Cooper's Hill is noted not just as a superb viewpoint, but also for the annual festival of cheese-rolling, which takes place on its excessively steep grass slope. The origins and antiquity of this event are unknown, but the festivities are now held on spring bank holiday Monday each year. Contestants plunge heroically from the maypole down the slope in pursuit of a mock cheese, the winner taking home a real 7lb (3kg) Double Gloucester as the prize. In about 500BC Cooper's Hill was part of a large Iron Age encampment.

Garden (accommodation, refreshments) has become something of an institution among Cotswold Way walkers, for refreshments and a warm welcome have been dispensed here since 1981. Beyond it the lane becomes a track, and the track a woodland path delving deeply into Witcombe Wood. (Out of the woods, below to the left, lie the remains of **Witcombe Roman Villa**, although this site is not on our route.)

WITCOMBE ROMAN VILLA

Witcombe Roman Villa stands on the spring-line near the foot of the northern slopes between Cooper's Hill and Birdlip. Dating from the first century AD the villa was built on land first exploited by Iron Age man, and excavations have unearthed sections of a bath house with fine mosaics depicting seascapes as well as fish. The villa is owned by English Heritage.

As with other extensive woodlands on this walk, an assortment of paths and tracks criss-cross among the trees. Again the correct Cotswold Way has been generously (though not too intrusively) waymarked. Simply make sure that the route you are following bears the distinctive CW acorn and arrow symbol. Eventually the path climbs out of the woods onto a road ascending Birdlip Hill. The continuing route crosses to a clear woodland track which rises to The Peak. For accommodation and refreshments, however, bear right on the road and walk uphill for about 400 metres to the village of

Birdlip, where accommodation and refreshments can be found (grid ref: 925144).

BIRDLIP

Birdlip stands on the edge of the Cotswold escarpment on the course of the Roman Ermin Street (or Ermin Way), which ran from Gloucester (Glevum) to Cirencester (Corinium), and is not to be confused with Ermine Street (or Way), which runs from London to Lincoln.

SECTION 9

Birdlip to Dowdeswell (A40)

Distance	9½ miles (15km)
Maps	Harvey's Cotswold Way 1:40,000
	OS Landranger 163 Cheltenham & Cirencester
	Area 1:50,000
	OS Explorer 179 Gloucester, Cheltenham &
	Stroud 1:25,000
Accommodation	Charlton Kings (+ ½ mile (800m)), and Dowdeswell
Refreshments	Near Crickley Hill, and at Dowdeswell

Once again woodlands are a major feature on this walk, but there are also wonderful open sections with uplifting, far-reaching views. History continues to have an impact too, but there are no villages at all on this section, just a few scattered buildings, and the odd intrusion of a busy road to remind you of the pleasures to be enjoyed in the more remote wolds elsewhere between Birdlip and Dowdeswell.

The day begins by rejoining the path as it crosses the slopes of Birdlip Hill and winds on a woodland track to a viewpoint on The Peak. You then follow a series of paths along the scarp edge, go over a busy road, and come on to Crickley Hill Country Park with its fascinating archaeological site and open grasslands speckled with orchids in springtime. From here the scarp is traced to Shurdington Hill, then along a former drove-road, followed by a return to the escarpment near Leckhampton Hill. Projecting from a lower terrace of the scarp is the Devil's Chimney, which has become the unofficial symbol of the Cotswold Way, although it's necessary to break off the path a little in order to see it close-to.

Beyond Leckhampton Hill the scarp is hugged again round Charlton Kings Common, before veering 'inland' to Seven Springs where a new route has been made to avoid a lengthy stretch of road-walking. The route gives more scenic pleasures from the scarp edge before descending through woodland to a valley in which lies Dowdeswell Reservoir.

Please see map,
Southbound,
Section 5.

Resume the route by taking the woodland track rising on the north side of the road below Birdlip. The track winds among trees and brings you to a path junction. Bear left and go on to another path junction. Bear left again for about 70 metres to the promontory viewpoint of The Peak, to enjoy the view, then backtrack to the junction and continue ahead (ignoring the previous path approaching from the right).

Leaving the woods, maintain direction along the left-hand edge of a field, then follow a switchback course along the scarp edge of Barrow Wake, with broad panoramas to enjoy as you walk. There are two topographs just above the waymarked path: one gives geological details, the other a panorama. The path eventually winds up to road-level. Continue ahead beside the busy A417 to reach the Air Balloon pub (grid ref: 935161) at a roundabout.

Cross the road with great care directly ahead, follow waymarks by the side of a building and bear left into woodland. Out of the trees you are now guided alongside a drystone wall as far as the promontory of **Crickley Hill**, with its Iron Age hill fort. Bear right along the scarp edge to an observation platform, continue through the car park (with public toilets and visitor centre) and by

CRICKLEY HILL

Crickley Hill is the site of one of the great archaeological discoveries of the Cotswolds. During the Neolithic period, some time between 4000–3000BC, more than 3 acres (1/ hectares) of the hill were occupied as a camp consisting of a single ditch and a bank. A second occupation took place in about 700BC when Iron Age settlers used 9 acres (3½ hectares) of the hill for housing, the storage of crops and livestock pens. A rampart and palisaded walkway surrounded this camp, and a 6ft (1.8m) ditch was dug. A third camp followed a period when Crickley Hill had been abandoned for some time by these first Iron Age settlers and, during this final occupation, round houses were built. This term of settlement is thought to have ended with destruction by fire. On the observation platform a series of information panels describe the site's fascinating history.

way of a wooden kissing gate into a meadow.

Walk along the right-hand edge of the meadow and through a narrow strip of beech woods. The waymarked path continues along the scarp edge to Shurdington Hill, where you come onto the old drove-road of Greenway Lane and turn right. As you walk along Greenway Lane the Devil's Chimney can be seen standing proud of the steep cut of the scarp half-left ahead. Our approach will double the actual crow-flying distance from here.

Greenway Lane leads to the B4070. Cross directly ahead and walk along a minor road that takes you past Ullenwood Manor. Beyond the manor's entrance, where the road curves to the right, break away left on a track next to a golf course. In inclement weather the lower part of this bridleway can be exceedingly muddy and water-logged. Follow the track uphill. It goes through a patch of woodland, passes behind a few secluded houses and brings you to a country lane (Hartley Lane). Turn left and wander downhill for perhaps 300 metres, keeping a lookout for a signpost indicating a narrow path that climbs among trees and shrubs on the right.

The path mounts the escarpment and eases along the scarp edge with fine views on the approach to Leckhampton Hill. Watch for a signed path on the left that goes downhill a short way to give a close view onto the **Devil's Chimney** (grid ref: 946184).

THE DEVIL'S CHIMNEY

One of the major landmark features of the Cotswold Way, the Devil's Chimney is a craggy finger of rock projecting from the scarp-face terrace below Leckhampton Hill. Throughout the 18th century extensive quarrying took place here, and the exposed pinnacle is a result of this industry. Local quarrymen apparently trimmed the chimney as part of a hoax. Although climbing the pinnacle is now prohibited, for many years it made a popular scramble, and the record apparently stands at 13 people on the top at one time!

Back on the main path continue over Leckhampton Hill, then along the scarp edge round Charlton Kings

The extravagance of a flower meadow in springtime – Charlton Kings Common

Note Should you be in need of liquid refreshment at this point, the Seven Springs Inn will be found a short distance down the A436 to the right.

Common heading first east, then south-east among gorse bushes and hollows where in the past ragstone was quarried. Lovely long views brighten the day. The path leads through a spinney and down an enclosed rectangular field, eventually coming onto a narrow road where you continue straight ahead (passing a windpump in the right-hand field) to reach the A435 a few paces north of the **Seven Springs** crossroads. ◄

Cross the road with great care and go through a gap in the drystone wall opposite. Walk straight ahead along the right headland of a large field, and on reaching the far corner cross a private road. Through a gate take a track rising into Wistley Grove. At the top of the slope turn left

SEVEN SPRINGS

Seven Springs is often claimed to be the source of the River Thames, although this is a moot point since it's the River Churn which begins here, and that is only a tributary of the Thames. The springs leak from the water table beneath Hartley Hill and may be found a short distance down the A436 in a tree-clad hollow north of the road.

on an enclosed path, which now leaves the wood and takes you round two sides of a large hilltop field, then along the scarp edge with huge views to enjoy. The way brings you alongside Wistley Plantation on Wistley Hill, where you then bear left near a seat that exploits the view, and take the continuing path that angles down the steep scarp slope to its bottom right-hand corner.

Pass through a gate and a group of trees, then walk down towards Old Dole Farm. On the way you come to a waymark post where you bear right to find another gate leading into Lineover Wood. Draped on the scarp slope this is an ancient woodland first mentioned in documents of the ninth century.

The path through Lineover Wood is obvious and waymarked. It makes a steady rising traverse, comes out through a gate and cuts round a field corner to another gate. It then descends along the boundary of a meadow before re-entering the wood to descend a number of timber-braced steps. The path continues to lose height, finally spilling out at the A40 almost opposite a tall grey building overlooking **Dowdeswell Reservoir**.

DOWDESWELL RESERVOIR

The reservoir was created in the late 19th century by damming the River Chelt upstream of Charlton Kings, in order to supply the needs of fast-growing Cheltenham. Despite its close proximity to the Cotswold Way, it is barely glimpsed by passing walkers.

Take the path on the left winding downhill below the road towards The Reservoir Inn. Just before the pub cross the A40 with great care, descend the slope beyond and turn right along a stony drive, or service road, leading to the reservoir. Cross a sluice and take the path alongside a cottage (Langett) which, at the time of writing, provides refreshments and accommodation for Cotswold Way walkers. (Please refer to the *CW Handbook & Accommodation List* for up-to-date information.)

SECTION 10

Dowdeswell (A40) to Cleeve Hill

Distance	6 miles (9½km)
Maps	Harvey's Cotswold Way 1:40,000
	OS Landranger 163 Cheltenham & Cirencester
	Area 1:50,000
	OS Explorer 179 Gloucester, Cheltenham &
	Stroud 1:25,000
Accommodation	Cleeve Hill and Bishop's Cleeve (+ 1½ miles (2½km))
Refreshments	None until Cleeve Hill

On this short stage the Cotswold Way crosses farmland on the way to the seemingly vast and breezy upland of Cleeve Common, the highest land on the route, which tops the 1000ft (300m) contour. Before fully mounting onto the common, the path weaves among gorse and hawthorn, lively with bird-life and butterflies, and provides numerous enticing views over the low country of patchwork fields and meadows. It's a fine stage and a lovely walk – but note that there are no refreshment facilities actually on the route, and that Cleeve Hill's opportunity, noted above, lies a short walk away from the path.

Please see map, Southbound, Section 4.

The path makes a steep climb alongside Dowdeswell Wood. It's a strenuous ascent, very slippery following wet weather, but eased in places by a series of steps. In springtime it's a delight of colour and birdsong (the wood is a nature reserve). At the top of the slope the path spills onto a narrow farm road beneath high-voltage power cables. There are kissing gates on either side of the road. Through the second of these cross a field half-right to the opposite boundary, which you then follow to the top of the field and another kissing gate that gives onto a very narrow lane (grid ref: 991211).

Continue straight ahead along a track which eventually brings you to a second narrow lane. Veer slightly left along this with its row of pollarded beech trees, taking the first turning on the left along another quiet country lane – this time through an avenue of mature beeches.

At the end of a small woodland on the right, leave the lane and walk alongside the trees, with a large meadow stretching away to your left, in order to reach the head of another narrow lane. Bear right through a gate and continue on a rising track to a region of disused quarries above to the right. Look for a waymark on a pole supporting overhead cables. This points you half-left down a brief slope for a few paces, then through a boundary on your right. A path now contours over a rough patch of hillside, weaving among gorse bushes as far as a four-way crossing. Bear left, still among gorse, and you will come to a stile over which you enter a butterfly reserve (the Bill Smyllie Reserve). The way through this is clear and easy, and you eventually leave it through a gate.

The way now skirts the lower edge of a beech wood, curves left, and goes down a slope alongside a fence. At a path junction turn right and begin the rising approach to Cleeve Common. This takes you through a gateway, then climbs (quite steeply in places) among clumps of hawthorn (waymarks guide you at junctions) and brings you to a gate leading onto **Cleeve Common**. Note the transmitter masts half-right ahead – they will appear and disappear with annoying frequency over the ensuing miles, and after making a lengthy tour of the common

From the western scarp edge of Cleeve Common, it's possible to look down on Nutterswood

CLEEVE COMMON

Cleeve Common contains the highest point of the Cotswolds at 1083ft (330m). The last expanse of unenclosed land in the region, it covers an area of about 3 square miles (7½ sq km) and is designated a grade 1 site of special scientific interest, with various orchids, glow-worms, and many different types of butterfly attracted by a range of habitats. In spite of the common's popularity with walkers and golfing enthusiasts, there are large areas that seem as remote as almost anywhere in Britain. Because of its height, this large upland plateau is often swept by mists, during which times it's a bleak and mysterious place.

you will find yourself very close to them again – having walked a 4 mile (6½km) circuit!

Wander ahead (slightly leftwards) to follow the scarp edge, first to the earthworks of an Iron Age hill fort, then beyond this along what is known as Cleeve Cloud, with Castle Rock showing ahead. Coming level with Castle Rock, waymarks send you away from the scarp, heading to the right over the golf course to a trig point vantage point at 1040ft (317m), where there's also a topograph indicating specific places of interest in the expansive panorama gained from here. Marker posts lead the continuing route in a devious descent until you come onto a clear path which leads towards the golf clubhouse.

Note that below Cleeve Hill, Bishop's Cleeve also has accommodation, including (at the time of writing) camping facilities.

The village of **Cleeve Hill** lies below, and those who have planned to spend the night there should break away and descend to the road (grid ref: 984268) to find accommodation and refreshments. ◀

CLEEVE HILL

Cleeve Hill is a very small village that seems to hang from the steep north-west slope of Cleeve Common, with notable views. Several Iron Age earthworks above the village tell of long-past settlements. One, known as the Ring, covers about ½ acre (⅕ hectare), and within it there's what may have been a hut platform. On Cleeve Common, Cleeve Hill Municipal Golf Course is owned by Tewkesbury Borough Council.

SECTION 11

Cleeve Hill to Winchcombe

Distance	6½ miles (10½km)
Maps	Harvey's Cotswold Way 1:40,000
	OS Landranger 163 Cheltenham & Cirencester Area 1:50,000
	OS Explorer 179 Gloucester, Cheltenham & Stroud, and OL45 The Cotswolds 1:25,000
Accommodation	Winchcombe
Refreshments	None until Winchcombe

The onward route continues the tour of Cleeve Common, a circuit that offers a constantly changing series of panoramas – in good conditions, that is. In inclement weather this high, exposed semi-moorland wears a very different face and, when the mists are swirling, one needs to be able to use a map and compass. In season a variety of orchids may be found here, together with a rich summer population of butterflies. However, this is only one aspect of the walk, for away from Cleeve Common there's once more an historic angle: Belas Knap is a splendid example of a Neolithic chambered tomb of the Severn-Cotswold Group, and the way enters its walled enclosure in order to give an opportunity to study it. Then there's the site of a Roman villa, only 100 metres or so off the path, and shortly before entering Winchcombe you catch sight of the 15th-century Sudeley Castle.

From Cleeve Hill the Cotswold Way leads round the northern edge of Cleeve Common, then cuts south over the 'empty' hinterland before drawing away again through a vast, open agricultural landscape and entering the drystone-walled compound of Belas Knap. Down then to Humblebee Woods, along a country lane, across the fields to Wadfield Farm and from there over more fields to Winchcombe. It's an interesting, varied walk, but with no opportunities for refreshment along the way.

From the clear path near the golf clubhouse on Cleeve Common, follow the waymark posts that lead to the right,

See map, South-bound, Section 3.

away from any obvious path, to rise over the golf course. On gaining a high point note the seat with a view, then, shortly after, you'll be swooping down south-eastward to the edge of a wall-enclosed woodland, with the Postlip Valley beyond.

Near the wood the path veers to the right and comes to a pond known as the Washpool (probably a sheep-dip). Beyond this cross a narrow cleave (dry valley) and climb its steep side on a stiff ascent heading south-east again. The gradient eases and the path continues. There are many cross-tracks, but waymark posts lead you roughly south, then south-east and south once more, keeping always well to the left of the transmitter towers. The path eventually takes you to a gate and away from Cleeve Common, where a very different landscape beckons.

A clear track now heads almost due east through large open fields beneath a line of high-voltage power cables, bringing you to a crossing track at Wontley Farm. Turn left and walk uphill and along the continuing track for a little over ½ mile (800m), then bear right through a gateway and follow a drystone wall ahead. This will bring you directly to **Belas Knap** Long Barrow (grid ref: 021255), one of the most impressive sites along the Cotswold Way. An information panel gives details.

Belas Knap above Winchcombe is one of many long barrows along the route of the Cotswold Way. When visiting, please treat it with respect

BELAS KNAP

Belas Knap is a very fine example of the chambered tombs, or long barrows, of the Severn-Cotswold Group, of which the Cotswold Way has visited many. The name means hilltop beacon, suggesting that the site was used by the Saxons (it stands above Winchcombe which was occupied during Saxon times). Of course Belas Knap existed long before the Saxons, for it dates from about 3000BC – a wedge-shaped mound measuring some 178ft (54m) long, 60ft (18m) wide, and about 13ft (4m) at its highest point. At its northern end there's a false portal with two horns lined with drystone walling and blocked by a massive slab. When excavated in 1863 the remains of five children and the skull of an adult were discovered behind it. There are two chambers along the eastern side, one on the west and another at the southern end, reached by way of shallow passages walled with stones laid in almost identical fashion to many of the drystone walls seen along the way. No less than 26 burials were found to have been made in the paired north-east and north-west chambers, and the remains of two males and two females in the south-eastern chamber.

Cross the stile into the walled enclosure and, having given time to study this impressive site, go out again by way of a kissing gate in the northern corner. Bear left and walk first alongside a woodland, then on the right-hand edge of a hilltop field with tremendous views. Enter a second, sloping field, at the bottom of which you bear left to find another kissing gate which takes you into woods and down to a country lane. (A short distance below this lane to the right a clump of conifers marks the site of **Wadfield Roman Villa**).

WADFIELD ROMAN VILLA

Wadfield Roman Villa is hidden from the Cotswold Way by a screen of conifers, but is representative of several Roman sites in the neighbourhood. Discovered in 1863 by a farm worker while ploughing, the site was excavated in 1894–5. On an exposed hillside overlooking the north-east, the villa consisted of a courtyard, at least two heated rooms, and two others with mosaic pavements. A shed on the site contains sections of floor mosaic.

SUDELEY CASTLE

Originally built in the 12th century, Sudeley Castle was rebuilt in 1440–50 by Ralph Boteler, who became lord chancellor and was made Baron Sudeley. Having created a magnificent building, he backed the wrong side in the Wars of the Roses and his property was confiscated by Edward IV. The castle eventually passed into the hands of Henry VIII, after whose death his widow, Katherine Parr, married Lord Seymour and came to live here. Shortly after giving birth in 1548 Katherine died and was buried in St Mary's Chapel. During the Civil War the castle was badly damaged, but the Elizabethan banqueting hall, tithe barn, Portmore Tower and St Mary's Chapel all survive from Boteler's time. The castle and grounds are open to the public.

There's always something to catch your eye along the Cotswold Way

Bear left along the lane for a very short distance to a junction. Go through a gate ahead and wander down a sloping meadow with Winchcombe seen in the valley below, the Vale of Evesham spreading beyond that, and the impressive **Sudeley Castle** off to the right. Out of the meadow go onto a drive and follow this to Corndean Lane. Along the lane pass a few houses, then go through a kissing gate on the right and keep ahead along the left-

WINCHCOMBE

The town has a number of archetypal Cotswold buildings in typical Cotswold stone. Once an important Saxon settlement, Winchcombe was the seat of Mercian royalty. Offa, King of Mercia, dedicated a nunnery here in AD790 and an abbey was established by his successor, Kenulf, in AD811. Kenulf had a son who was murdered at the behest of his ambitious sister, and as a consequence of Kenelm's death assorted miracles were attributed to him which, in turn, made the town a place of pilgrimage. The abbey has gone, but the Parish Church of St Peter, built in the 15th century, owes something to abbey money which helped pay for its construction. Among its more notable features are the 40 gargoyles that adorn the outer walls. Elsewhere in the town you will find a pair of wooden stocks outside the Folk Museum, and among its buildings some fine old inns, Tudor houses and cottages. Tourist information: Town Hall, High Street, Winchcombe ☎01242 602925.

hand edge of a field. On coming to a second kissing gate maintain direction across a meadow to its far left-hand corner where you come onto a road. Turn left, cross the little River Isbourne and walk up Vineyard Street into **Winchcombe**, arriving near the Church of St Peter (grid ref: 024282). Winchcombe is a pleasant small town with a range of accommodation, pubs, restaurants, shops, a post office and so on.

SECTION 12

Winchcombe to Stanton

Distance	8 miles (12½km)
Maps	Harvey's Cotswold Way 1:40,000
	OS Landranger 150 Worcester, The Malverns &
	Surrounding Area 1:50,000
	OS Explorer OL45 The Cotswolds 1:25,000
Accommodation	Hailes, Wood Stanway, Stanway and Stanton
Refreshments	Hailes and Stanton

Much of this penultimate stage wanders below the scarp face, although above Hailes Abbey the Cotswold Way climbs onto the Wolden escarpment for a short spell before dropping down the slope again. This is a peaceful walk, a gentle lowland treasure of long views and tiny villages, of superb specimen trees and individual buildings that make you pause and wonder.

The route takes you through Winchcombe into quiet farmland, across a former salt way and by the side of the ruins of Hailes Abbey (which had a 500-year chequered history and is worth a brief visit). From Hailes the route goes into orchard country and up to yet another hill fort site before coming onto an old drove-road leading to Stumps Cross. Down then to Wood Stanway tucked against the hill, and across more fields to the tiny village of Stanway, with its Jacobean gatehouse, 12th-century church, great tithe barn and lovely thatched cricket pavilion set upon staddle stones. The continuing path cuts through the stately parkland of Stanway House, over a handful of low-lying fields and into one of the loveliest of all Cotswold villages. Stanton is the prime lure on this stage. It beckons unseen across the fields, and has the effect of elevating the walk to a truly memorable outing – even without the day's other attributes, which in themselves ought not to be lightly dismissed.

Please see map, Southbound, Section 2.

Entering Winchcombe from Vineyard Street, turn right and walk through the town along the B4632. On the northern outskirts the road swings right and then left to

A cottage in Stanton

cross the River Isbourne. Soon after this you leave it and turn right along Puck Pit Lane. At first metalled, the lane becomes an enclosed track. When it ends, cross a stile and walk across a field to a footbridge, and then continue heading north-east over a series of undulating fields, linked by gates and guided by waymarks, until you come to a track. Bear left and the track will take you to Salter's Lane (grid ref: 047301) on the outskirts of Hailes (accommodation). Turn right along this one-time saltway (which linked Droitwich with the Thames Valley) for about 100 metres.

Leave Salter's Lane by turning left on a drive alongside a house named The Barn, then take a footpath angling across a meadow to its far right-hand corner where you come onto a country road next to the ruins of **Hailes Abbey**, some of which can be seen over the boundary hedge.

Turn right and walk along the road. When it forks, note that refreshments can be found by taking the right branch to Hayles Fruit Farm. For the continuing Cotswold Way, take the left branch ahead on a track rising between Hailes Wood and orchards. Soon after the wood ends, a stile by

HAILES ABBEY

Managed and maintained by English Heritage Hailes Abbey was built in the 13th century by Richard, Earl of Cornwall and brother of Henry III, as a thanksgiving for having survived a near-shipwreck. The abbey was consecrated in 1251 for a community of Cistercian monks, and when a phial said to contain the blood of Christ was presented by Richard's second son, Edmund, in 1270, Hailes became a place of pilgrimage for nearly 300 years. But in 1538 the phial was taken to London for analysis and the contents pronounced as nothing more than 'honey clarified and coloured with saffron'. The following year, during the dissolution of the monasteries, the abbey was closed, its ornaments taken away, and the buildings sold to a private dealer in 1542. Now only the ivy-clad archways, crumbling masonry and clearly defined foundations remain. Nearby, on the opposite side of the lane, stands the 12th-century Church of St Nicholas, with a number of medieval wall paintings that make the building also worthy of a visit.

a signpost directs you into the left-hand meadow. There is little to be seen of a footpath on the ground, but the way leads diagonally up the slope towards a clump of trees reached through meadows linked by gates. The final climb to the top of the slope is steep, and leads to the spot from where it is said Thomas Cromwell watched the dismantling of Hailes Abbey. A gate gives access onto **Beckbury Camp**, another of the many Cotswold hill forts (grid ref: 064299).

BECKBURY CAMP

To the east of Hailes Abbey, Beckbury Camp is the site of another Iron Age hill fort of more than 4 acres (1½ hectares). It consisted of a single ditch and rampart, but the ditch has since been filled, although along the east side of the rampart its position can still be identified. Located on the scarp edge, the site would have been comparatively easy to defend.

Turn left to walk along the field boundary, with big views into the Vale of Evesham, then bear right at the far side, still along the left-hand margin of the field. Pass through a gap in the wall and resume direction towards a little woodland where you come onto a crossing track (a former sheep drove-road). Bear left along the track (known as Campden Lane) for about ½ mile (800m), passing on the way a few farm buildings and a sorry-looking corrugated-iron shed on staddle stones.

The track brings you to the B4077 at Stumps Cross (grid ref: 076304). Do not go onto the road; instead, turn left round a wall, go through a gate and follow the left-hand wall heading north-east to the lip of the escarpment at the end of a line of trees. Here there is a seat with a view. Now descend the slope to pass well to the left of a house, then cross several meadows linked by waymarked gates or stiles to a track by Glebe Farm. Passing the farm to your left continue down the track and onto a metalled road in the farming hamlet of Wood Stanway (accommodation).

Turn right past Wood Stanway House, walk along the left-hand boundaries of successive low-lying fields, and emerge onto the B4077 once more on the outskirts

Wandering through Stanway, the route passes the Church of St Peter

of Stanway (sometimes known as Church Stanway to avoid confusion with Wood Stanway). Go left for about 40 metres, turn right to cross a small meadow, then continue on a footpath which brings you past a blacksmith's workshop and the remains of a watermill, and then onto another narrow lane in the hamlet of **Stanway** (accommodation).

STANWAY

Church Stanway as it's also known, is little more than a clutch of buildings in the shadow, so to speak, of the Jacobean manor, Stanway House. There's an air of feudalism about it – the church, the houses, even the trees appear to come under manorial patronage. In almost 1300 years of ownership, the manor has changed hands only once (apart from inheritance, that is), so perhaps it's not surprising that the community should appear so closely knit. As well as the manor and 12th-century Church of St Peter (with much Victorian reconstruction), note the massive tithe barn, the three-storeyed Jacobean gatehouse with gables adorned with scallop shell finials, and the 13th-century watermill that once belonged to the abbots of Tewkesbury.

Bear right and follow the lane as it swings first past the fanciful gatehouse of Stanway House, then the church next door. Soon after this, note through the private gateway to Stanway House, a lovely old tithe barn on the right, and in the meadow on the left an attractive thatched cricket pavilion set upon staddle stones.

A stile on the right, found soon after passing the entrance to Stanway House, takes you into parkland which you cross among stately oaks and chestnut trees. Waymark posts guide the route, for otherwise there are few signs of a path. Leave the parkland at its north-east corner and follow the continuing footpath over several fields skirting the foot of the slope. A broad panorama lies ahead and to the left, while the village of Stanton draws you on. At last enter the village near a corrugated-iron Dutch barn, and bear left on a farm drive. This leads to a road where you turn right (grid ref: 067341) into the heart of lovely **Stanton** (accommodation, refreshments).

STANTON

Stanton has been called 'the perfect Cotswold village', and not without good reason. The mellow, honey-coloured stone, the sometimes uneven gabled roofs of its cottages, the walls overhung with flowering plants, the lovely Church of St Michael with its slender spire, and the medieval market cross – all these, and more, lend the village an air almost of unreality.

Stanton was originally little more than a group of 16th-century cottages and farmhouses built from local stone, but in such a sympathetic manner that they seem now to have grown straight out of the ground. When Sir Philip Stott came to Stanton Court in 1906, however, he found the village rather neglected, and from then until his death in 1937 he spent much money and architectural talent on restoring it to the splendour we see today. It is one of the glories of the Cotswold Way.

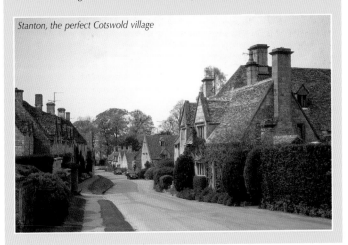

Stanton, the perfect Cotswold village

SECTION 13

Stanton to Chipping Campden

Distance	10 miles (16km)
Maps	Harvey's Cotswold Way 1:40,000
	OS Landranger 150 Worcester, The Malverns &
	Surrounding Area, and 151 Stratford-upon-Avon &
	Surrounding Area 1:50,000
	OS Explorer OL45 The Cotswolds 1:25,000
Accommodation	Broadway and Chipping Campden
Refreshments	Broadway and Chipping Campden

As the final stage of the long walk from Bath, this is something of an up and down course, perhaps a little strenuous on account of the height to be gained and lost, but full of variety and interest. There are some fine long views to draw the eye, easy tracks on the rim of the escarpment, the much-lauded village of Broadway to explore, Broadway Tower to visit and, at the end of it all, glorious Chipping Campden to underscore the pleasures of 102 miles (164km) of Cotswold wayfaring.

The splendours of Stanton lead directly to an uphill route where meadows and woodland clumps adorn the slopes of Shenberrow Hill. On the escarpment yet another hill fort is to be found. Heading north along a track with a view the Vale of Evesham swallows distance far below. The way then brings you down to woods and fields and into the crowded streets of Broadway. There's no peace to be had here, but the lovely buildings that line the wide main street hold your interest until it's time to climb again, this time to Broadway Tower, from where it's claimed you can see 12 counties on a clear day. Attempting to put names to features in that vast panorama is likely to involve much argument and speculation. Better to remain ignorant and simply enjoy the view! From Broadway Tower to Fish Hill is a green, undulating walk of little distance. Next follows a level stretch of arable farmland, then along the Mile Drive and onto Dover's Hill for the last big view of the walk, before slipping innocently into Chipping Campden, a market town without equal and an elegant finish to an uplifting experience.

Stanton is so small a village that to walk straight through would occupy only a few short minutes, though to do so would be insensitive. This is a community to treasure, with streets to stroll along at an unhurried pace, cottages with roses over doorways to admire, and the wolds rising behind as if to offer protection.

Please see map, Southbound, Section One.

So, amble along the street (Manorway) on entering, then swing sharp right where it forks, to pass the old market cross. The street forks again – should you need refreshment, keep straight ahead to find the Mount Inn, otherwise bear right and wander up to a delightful thatched cottage where you veer left and follow a track that rises out of the village. Keep on the track until a

The medieval market cross in Stanton

waymark directs you to the right through a gate by a pond (Stanton Reservoir). Work your way round and above the left-hand side of the reservoir, staying close to the right-hand boundary of a sloping meadow, and then go into the adjacent field. Resume direction, but now with the field boundary on your left, and crossing a stile come to a tight cleave, or dry valley, among trees.

Go up the cleave to Shenberrow Hill, where you bear left past a farm by a hill fort, and follow the track ahead. This takes you beside Long Hill Plantation on the scarp edge, then curves to the right to a cattlegrid and a junction of tracks. Bear left then right on a continuing track. ◀

Views begin to extend out to the west as you wander along this escarpment track. It's easy walking, with no route-finding problems, just long views and cloudscapes, with flowers at your feet and birds singing from the wayside scrub and crowns of trees.

The track then begins to lose height and brings you to a cluster of farm buildings on the edge of Buckland Wood. Bear left now on a continuation of the track heading north for nearly ½ mile (800m). Over a stile on the right you approach a barn – which sits astride the county boundaries of Gloucestershire and Hereford and Worcester – and make a right-hand detour round it.

Having passed the barn on your left, resume direction along the right headland of a field at the far side of which you enter Broadway Coppice. Descend through this little woodland of hazel, oak, birch and ash, and when you emerge Broadway Tower can be seen on a hill crest to the north-east. Continue down the slope to an enclosed path which takes you onto the narrow West End Lane (grid ref: 090371).

Cross the lane and continue directly ahead through linking fields and over a footbridge. Soon come onto a track (or drive) leading into Church Street, almost opposite the Parish Church of St Michael and All Angels in **Broadway** (accommodation, refreshments). Turn left and wander down the street to the green, then bear right to walk through Broadway's busy High Street.

Shenberrow Hill above Stanton is the site of yet another Iron Age hill fort, of about 2½ acres (1 hectare), which was excavated in 1935. Of the various artefacts revealed, there were pieces of pottery, a bronze bracelet and two bone needles.

BROADWAY

The quintessential Cotswold village, Broadway is much larger than Stanton, and lined with handsome shops, cottages and hotels on a wide street (hence 'broad way'). It is said to have been 'discovered' by William Morris, in whose wake came a number of Victorian artists to further extend its fame. The village grew in importance during the era of the stagecoach by providing accommodation and a change of horses in readiness for the steep haul up Fish Hill. Nowadays horses have been replaced by horsepower, and Broadway is at times a snarl of traffic amid a clutter of commerce. Without traffic the village is a gem, with wisteria-clad cottages, 17th-century almshouses, an avenue of red-flowering chestnut trees, a village green and two churches, the oldest of which is St Eadburgh's, dating from the 12th century. Tourist information: Cotswold Court, The Green, Broadway ☎01386 852937.

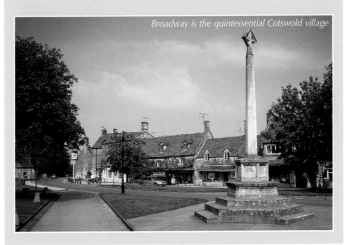

Broadway is the quintessential Cotswold village

There's much to admire and enjoy as you wander through, although the unrestrained commercialism tends to jar by comparison with Stanton's simplicity. However, if it's refreshment you need, Broadway's the place. There are also shops in which to restock, if necessary, for the remaining few miles of the walk.

Broadway lies at the foot of the scarp slope

Keep along the main street, passing the major junction where Leamington Road turns north, and almost 200 yards (metres) beyond that, turn right on a signed drive-cum-farm track. Go through a gate, across a paddock to another gate, then bear half-left where the way now progresses uphill through meadows linked by kissing gates or stiles towards **Broadway Tower**. Shortly before you reach the tower the path is enclosed by fences.

BROADWAY TOWER

Broadway Tower is set upon a grassy knoll from which it commands a tremendous panoramic view over the Vale of Evesham. At 1089ft (332m) the top of the tower is (just) the highest point in the Cotswolds (Cleeve Common's high ground measures 1083ft (330m)). Designed by James Wyatt in 1798 for the sixth Earl of Coventry, the tower is a Norman-style keep with three rounded turrets. Around it lies part of the Broadway Tower Country Park, in which the Tower Barn is about 150 years old, while Rookery Barn houses an information centre and restaurant.

Access to the country park is on the right, while the Cotswold Way breaks to the left through a gate and advances across a rough undulating pasture. Go through another gate and wander down a shallow cleave beyond which you enter woodland. Follow the footpath winding through, and when you leave the woodland continue on a track which curves to the right behind a house (the former Fish Inn) and onto a tarmac service road with a quarry on your right. So come to the A44 at the top of Fish Hill (grid ref 120368).

Cross the road with great care and go through a gap in the wall opposite a toilet block at the Fish Hill picnic site. Bear left following waymarks up a grass slope through the picnic area, and then turn right at the top just before a topograph. Through a gate the continuing path takes you across a field to a country road, Buckle Street. Maintain direction over two more fields, then through a gap in a drystone wall to join the Mile Drive.

Wander ahead along the broad grassy avenue of the Mile Drive, crossing a farm drive midway, and at the far end go briefly through a spinney and out again by way of another gap in a drystone wall. Come onto a country road and bear right for about 400 metres or so (there's a spacious grass verge for safe walking), passing the Kiftsgate Stone on the left which marks the site of an ancient meeting place. On coming to a minor cross-roads turn left, soon after which you arrive at a National Trust car park giving access to **Dover's Hill** on the right.

DOVER'S HILL

Dover's Hill is the last of the many fine vantage points for the northbound Cotswold Way walker. At 755ft (230m) it was named after Captain Robert Dover (1582–1652), a wealthy and somewhat eccentric lawyer who organised his first 'Olympick Games' there in 1612. The games included leapfrog, wrestling, skittles and 'shin-kicking', and apart from an interruption during the Civil War they continued annually until 1852. Dover's Olympics were revived in 1951, and now take place each spring bank holiday.

Walk ahead to a topograph, then wander along the edge of the escarpment with lovely views into the Vale of Evesham to the left. When you reach a trig point bear right to find a kissing gate in the meadow corner. With your back to the last extensive panorama of the walk, follow a path between fields to Kingcomb Lane.

Cross the road, turn left and, after about 100 metres, head to the right on a descending path which comes onto a track. This becomes the metalled Hoo Lane further down and brings you to a junction by a thatched cottage. Continue ahead, then turn left by St Catherine's Roman Catholic Church into **Chipping Campden** High Street. Continue ahead, passing Sheep Street on the right, then the Town Hall (the official end to the Cotswold Way), and many other lovely buildings, before turning right into Church Street. Walk the last few hundred metres to the Parish Church of St James, thus completing your 102 mile (164km) pilgrimage from Bath Abbey.

The Market Hall in Chipping Campden, built in 1627, is a prominent feature of the High Street

204

CHIPPING CAMPDEN

This is a worthy town in which to finish the Cotswold Way. Like so many others visited along the route, its elegance stems from the wool trade. The open-sided Market Hall, built in 1627, is an eye-catching feature, and nearby the 14th-century Woolstaplers' Hall houses the town's museum, while opposite stands Grevel House, dating from 1380. William Grevel, whose home it was, has a large memorial brass in the Parish Church of St James, reckoned to be one of the finest examples of a Cotswold 'wool church'. Next to it stand the fanciful gateway and onion-topped lodges that mark the entrance to one-time Campden House, built by Sir Baptist Hicks for an unbelievable £29,000 in 1615. Thirty years later it was burned down by Royalist troops during the Civil War. Alongside Church Street, on a raised pavement, stands a row of attractive almshouses, also built by Hicks, but for a more modest £1000, to house 12 of the local poor. Chipping Campden has a range of accommodation, restaurants, pubs, shops, a post office, and so on, and there are buses to Stratford-upon-Avon for the nearest rail link. Tourist information: Old Police Station, High Street, Chipping Campden ☎01386 841206.

Chipping Campden High Street

Shake the dust from your boots and be thankful for these days of exercise and beauty. Congratulations on your achievement!

National trail signpost, Tormarton

APPENDIX A

USEFUL ADDRESSES

The Cotswold Way National Trail
Office
The Malthouse
Standish
Stonehouse
Gloucestershire GL10 3DL
☎01453 827004
cotsway@gloscc.gov.uk
www.nationaltrail.co.uk

Cotswolds AONB
The Old Police Station
Cotswold Heritage Centre
Northleach
Gloucestershire GL54 3JH
☎01451 862000
www.cotswoldsaonb.com

The Ramblers' Association
2nd Floor
Camelford House
87–90 Albert Embankment
London SE1 7TW
☎020 7339 8500
ramblers@ramblers.org.uk
www.ramblers.org.uk

Tourist Information Offices
Abbey Chambers
Abbey Churchyard
Bath
☎0906 711 2000 (premium rates)

1 Cotswold Court
The Green
Broadway
Worcestershire WR12
☎01386 852937

77 The Promenade
Cheltenham
Gloucestershire
☎01242 522878
www.visitcheltenham.gov.uk

The Old Police Station
High Street
Chipping Campden
Gloucestershire GL55
☎01386 841206
www.chippingcampden.co.uk

The Library
Stroud Road
Painswick
Gloucestershire GL6
☎01452 813522

The Subscription Rooms
George Street
Stroud
Gloucestershire
☎01453 760960
www.stroud.gov.uk

The Heritage Centre
The Chipping
Wotton-under-Edge
Gloucestershire GL12
☎01453 521541
www.wottonheritage.com

The Town Hall
High Street
Winchcombe
Gloucestershire GL54
☎01242 602925

Morris dancers in Bath (Section 13 southbound, Section 1 northbound)

APPENDIX B

PUBLIC TRANSPORT INFORMATION

For information about rail travel, timetables and fares, contact National Rail Enquiries ☎0845 748 4950, **www.rail.co.uk** or **www.nationalrail.co.uk**. Bookings can be made online via **www.qjump.co.uk** or **www.thetrainline.com**

For bus travel try Traveline ☎0870 608 2608, **www.traveline.org.uk**
The National Express bus network can be contacted on ☎0870 580 8080

West of Cold Ashton, Greenway Lane works its way through an enticing landscape (Section 13 southbound, Section 1 northbound)

APPENDIX C

RECOMMENDED FURTHER READING

Cotswolds – Leisure Guide (AA/Ordnance Survey, 1986)

The Cotswold Way Handbook (Ramblers' Association)

Brill, Edith, *Portrait of the Cotswolds* (Hale, 1971)

        Life and Tradition in the Cotswolds (Dent, 1973)

Crosher, G. R., *Along the Cotswold Ways* (Cassell, 1976)

Finberg, H. P. R., *The Gloucestershire Landscape* (Hodder & Stoughton, 1975)

Hadfield, C. & A. M., *The Cotswolds: A New Study* (David & Charles, 1967)

Hill, S., *Spirit of the Cotswolds* (Michael Joseph, 1988)

Lewis, J., *Walking the Cotswold Way* (David & Charles, 1986)

Pevsner, N., *The Buildings of England: Worcestershire* (Penguin, 1968)

Richards, M., *The Cotswold Way* (Thornhill Press, 1999)

        The Cotswold Way (Penguin, 1984)

Sale, R., *A Guide to the Cotswold Way* (Constable, 1980)

        A Visitor's Guide to the Cotswolds (Moorland Publishing, 1982)

Smith, B., *The Cotswolds* (Batsford, 1976)

Verey, D. *The Buildings of England: Gloucestershire, The Cotswolds* (Penguin 1979)

        Cotswold Churches (Batsford, 1976)

Wright, L. & Priddey, D., *Cotswold Heritage* (Hale, 1979)

APPENDIX D

SECTION BY SECTION SOUTHWARDS

Section 1
Chipping Campden to Stanton
Distance: 10 miles (16km)
Passes through Broadway and Stanton

Section 2
Stanton to Winchcombe
Distance: 8 miles (12½km)
Passes through Stanway, Wood Stanway and Winchcombe

Section 3
Winchcombe to Cleeve Hill
Distance: 6½ miles (10½km)
Passes through no villages, but comes close to Cleeve Hill

Kelston Round Hill, from Prospect Stile
(Section 13 southbound, Section 1 northbound)

Section 4
Cleeve Hill to Dowdeswell (A40)
Distance: 6 miles (9½km)
Passes through no villages

Section 5
Dowdeswell (A40) to Birdlip
Distance: 9½ miles (15km)
Passes through no villages, but comes close to Birdlip

Section 6
Birdlip to Painswick
Distance: 7 miles (11km)
Passes through Cooper's Hill and Painswick

Section 7
Painswick to Middleyard (King's Stanley)
Distance: 9½ miles (15km)
Passes near Edge and King's Stanley, and through Middleyard

Section 8
Middleyard (King's Stanley) to Dursley
Distance: 6½ miles (10½km)
Passes through Dursley

Section 9
Dursley to Wotton-under-Edge
Distance: 7 miles (11km)
Passes through North Nibley and Wotton-under-Edge

Section 10
Wotton-under-Edge to Hawkesbury Upton
Distance: 8 miles (12½km)
Passes near Wortley, and through Alderley, Lower Kilcott and Hawkesbury Upton

Section 11
Hawkesbury Upton to Tormarton
Distance: 8 miles (12½km)
Passes through Horton, Little Sodbury, Old Sodbury and Tormarton

Section 12
Tormarton to Cold Ashton
Distance: 6 miles (9½km)
Passes through Dyrham, Pennsylvania and Cold Ashton

Section 13
Cold Ashton to Bath
Distance: 10 miles (16km)
Passes through Weston and Bath

Alderley church; a peaceful setting for a tiny village (Section 10 southbound, Section 4 northbound)

APPENDIX E

SECTION BY SECTION NORTHWARDS

Section 1
Bath to Cold Ashton
Distance: 10 miles (16km)
Passes through Weston and Cold Ashton

Section 2
Cold Ashton to Tormarton
Distance: 6 miles (9½km)
Passes through Pennsylvania, Dyrham and Tormarton

Section 3
Tormarton to Hawkesbury Upton
Distance: 8 miles (12½km)
Passes through Old Sodbury, Little Sodbury, Horton and Hawkesbury Upton

The Royal Crescent, Bath

Section 4
Hawkesbury Upton to Wotton-under-Edge
Distance: 8 miles (12½km)
Passes through Lower Kilcott and Alderley, near Wortley and through Wotton-under-Edge

Section 5
Wotton-under-Edge to Dursley
Distance: 7 miles (11km)
Passes through North Nibley and Dursley

Section 6
Dursley to Middleyard (King's Stanley)
Distance: 6½ miles (10½km)
Passes through Middleyard and comes close to King's Stanley

Section 7
Middleyard (King's Stanley) to Painswick
Distance: 9½ miles (15km)
Passes close to Edge, and through Painswick

Section 8
Painswick to Birdlip
Distance: 7 miles (11km)
Passes through Cooper's Hill and comes close to Birdlip

Section 9
Birdlip to Dowdeswell (A40)
Distance: 9½ miles (15km)
Passes through no villages

Section 10
Dowdeswell (A40) to Cleeve Hill
Distance: 6 miles (9½km)
Passes through no villages, but comes close to Cleeve Hill

Section 11
Cleeve Hill to Winchcombe
Distance: 6½ miles (10½km)
Passes through Winchcombe

Seductive landscapes and generous skies – the north-west side of Dyrham Park
(Section 12 southbound, Section 2 northbound)

Section 12

Winchcombe to Stanton
Distance: 8 miles (12½km)
Passes through Wood Stanway, Stanway and Stanton

Section 13

Stanton to Chipping Campden
Distance: 10 miles (16km)
Passes through Broadway and Chipping Campden

NOTES

NOTES

NOTES

LISTING OF CICERONE GUIDES

BACKPACKING
The End to End Trail
Three Peaks, Ten Tors
Backpacker's Britain Vol 1 –
  Northern England
Backpacker's Britain Vol 2 – Wales
Backpacker's Britain Vol 3 –
  Northern Scotland
The Book of the Bivvy

**NORTHERN ENGLAND
LONG-DISTANCE TRAILS**
The Dales Way
The Reiver's Way
The Alternative Coast to Coast
A Northern Coast to Coast Walk
The Pennine Way
Hadrian's Wall Path
The Teesdale Way

FOR COLLECTORS OF SUMMITS
The Relative Hills of Britain
Mts England & Wales Vol 2 –
  England
Mts England & Wales Vol 1 – Wales

UK GENERAL
The National Trails

BRITISH CYCLE GUIDES
The Cumbria Cycle Way
Lands End to John O'Groats – Cycle
  Guide
Rural Rides No.1 – West Surrey
Rural Rides No.2 – East Surrey
South Lakeland Cycle Rides
Border Country Cycle Routes
Lancashire Cycle Way

CANOE GUIDES
Canoeist's Guide to the North-East

**LAKE DISTRICT AND
MORECAMBE BAY**
Coniston Copper Mines
Scrambles in the Lake District
  (North)
Scrambles in the Lake District
  (South)
Walks in Silverdale and
  Arnside AONB
Short Walks in Lakeland 1 – South
Short Walks in Lakeland 2 – North
Short Walks in Lakeland 3 – West
The Tarns of Lakeland Vol 1 – West
The Tarns of Lakeland Vol 2 – East
The Cumbria Way &
  Allerdale Ramble
Lake District Winter Climbs
Roads and Tracks of the Lake
  District
The Lake District Angler's Guide
Rocky Rambler's Wild Walks
An Atlas of the English Lakes
Tour of the Lake District
The Cumbria Coastal Way

NORTH-WEST ENGLAND
Walker's Guide to the
  Lancaster Canal
Family Walks in the
  Forest Of Bowland

Walks in Ribble Country
Historic Walks in Cheshire
Walking in Lancashire
Walks in Lancashire Witch Country
The Ribble Way

THE ISLE OF MAN
Walking on the Isle of Man
The Isle of Man Coastal Path

**PENNINES AND
NORTH-EAST ENGLAND**
Walks in the Yorkshire Dales
Walks on the North York Moors,
  books 1 and 2
Walking in the South Pennines
Walking in the North Pennines
Walking in the Wolds
Waterfall Walks – Teesdale and High
  Pennines
Walking in County Durham
Yorkshire Dales Angler's Guide
Walks in Dales Country
Historic Walks in North Yorkshire
South Pennine Walks
Walking in Northumberland
Cleveland Way and Yorkshire Wolds
  Way
The North York Moors

**DERBYSHIRE, PEAK DISTRICT,
EAST MIDLANDS**
High Peak Walks
White Peak Walks Northern Dales
White Peak Walks Southern Dales
Star Family Walks Peak District &
  South Yorkshire
Walking In Peakland
Historic Walks in Derbyshire

WALES AND WELSH BORDERS
Ascent of Snowdon
Welsh Winter Climbs
Hillwalking in Wales – Vol 1
Hillwalking in Wales – Vol 2
Scrambles in Snowdonia
Hillwalking in Snowdonia
The Ridges of Snowdonia
Hereford & the Wye Valley
Walking Offa's Dyke Path
Lleyn Peninsula Coastal Path
Anglesey Coast Walks
The Shropshire Way
Spirit Paths of Wales
Glyndwr's Way
The Pembrokeshire Coastal Path
Walking in Pembrokeshire
The Shropshire Hills – A Walker's
  Guide

MIDLANDS
The Cotswold Way
The Grand Union Canal Walk
Walking in Warwickshire
Walking in Worcestershire
Walking in Staffordshire
Heart of England Walks

SOUTHERN ENGLAND
Exmoor & the Quantocks
Walking in the Chilterns

Walking in Kent
Two Moors Way
Walking in Dorset
A Walker's Guide to the Isle of
  Wight
Walking in Somerset
The Thames Path
Channel Island Walks
Walking in Buckinghamshire
The Isles of Scilly
Walking in Hampshire
Walking in Bedfordshire
The Lea Valley Walk
Walking in Berkshire
The Definitive Guide to
  Walking in London
The Greater Ridgeway
Walking on Dartmoor
The South West Coast Path
Walking in Sussex
The North Downs Way
The South Downs Way

SCOTLAND
Scottish Glens 1 – Cairngorm Glens
Scottish Glens 2 – Atholl Glens
Scottish Glens 3 – Glens of
  Rannoch
Scottish Glens 4 – Glens of Trossach
Scottish Glens 5 – Glens of Argyll
Scottish Glens 6 – The Great Glen
Scottish Glens 7 – The Angus Glens
Scottish Glens 8 – Knoydart
  to Morvern
Scottish Glens 9 – The Glens
  of Ross-shire
The Island of Rhum
Torridon – A Walker's Guide
Walking the Galloway Hills
Border Pubs & Inns –
  A Walkers' Guide
Scrambles in Lochaber
Walking in the Hebrides
Central Highlands: 6 Long
  Distance Walks
Walking in the Isle of Arran
Walking in the Lowther Hills
North to the Cape
The Border Country –
  A Walker's Guide
Winter Climbs – Cairngorms
The Speyside Way
Winter Climbs – Ben Nevis &
  Glencoe
The Isle of Skye, A Walker's Guide
The West Highland Way
Scotland's Far North
Walking the Munros Vol 1 –
  Southern, Central
Walking the Munros Vol 2 –
  Northern & Cairngorms
Scotland's Far West
Walking in the Cairngorms
Walking in the Ochils, Campsie
  Fells and Lomond Hills
Scotland's Mountain Ridges
The Great Glen Way

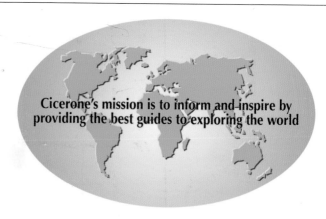

Cicerone's mission is to inform and inspire by providing the best guides to exploring the world

Since its foundation over 30 years ago, Cicerone has specialised in publishing guidebooks and has built a reputation for quality and reliability. It now publishes nearly 300 guides to the major destinations for outdoor enthusiasts, including Europe, UK and the rest of the world.

Written by leading and committed specialists, Cicerone guides are recognised as the most authoritative. They are full of information, maps and illustrations so that the user can plan and complete a successful and safe trip or expedition – be it a long face climb, a walk over Lakeland fells, an alpine traverse, a Himalayan trek or a ramble in the countryside.

With a thorough introduction to assist planning, clear diagrams, maps and colour photographs to illustrate the terrain and route, and accurate and detailed text, Cicerone guides are designed for ease of use and access to the information.

If the facts on the ground change, or there is any aspect of a guide that you think we can improve, we are always delighted to hear from you.

Cicerone Press
2 Police Square Milnthorpe Cumbria LA7 7PY
Tel:01539 562 069   Fax:01539 563 417
e-mail:info@cicerone.co.uk   web:www.cicerone.co.uk